Imagine
Japan
A Memorable Journey

Imagin
Japa

ing
n

A Memorable Journey

Text by **James M. Vardaman**
IBC Publishing

© 2015 IBC Publishing, Inc.

All photographs by Aflo Co., Ltd. except:
page 110: Rokuon-ji
page 111: Jisho-ji

Published by IBC Publishing, Inc.
Ryoshu Kagurazaka Bldg. 9F, 29-3 Nakazato-cho
Shinjuku-ku, Tokyo 162-0804

www.ibcpub.co.jp

All rights reserved. No part of this book may be
reproduced in any form without written permission from the publisher.

First Edition 2015
Third Printing January 2020
ISBN 978-4-7946-0346-3
Printed in Japan

Contents

Foreword — 6 – 7

Map of Japan — 8 – 9

Hokkaido — 11 – 28

Tohoku — 29 – 52

Kanto — 53 – 84

Chubu — 85 – 104

Kinki — 105 – 136

Chugoku — 137 – 150

Shikoku — 151 – 158

Kyushu — 159 – 178

Okinawa — 179 – 191

Foreword   A Culture of Nature

Regardless of how one approaches Japan, it soon becomes apparent that the culture of its people is inextricably linked with the natural world. This is not to say that other cultures do not reflect the natural environment in many ways, but the degree of sensitivity to nature seems particularly strong in Japanese culture.

Works of literature from the *Kojiki* to the *Tale of Genji* to the novels of Kawabata Yasunari employ images of nature not only to place the timing of events, but also to imply the moods of the protagonists and the meaning of their actions. The poetry of the *Man'yoshu* and the haiku of Matsuo Basho could not have been written and cannot be fully comprehended without considering the consensual understanding of particular flowers, trees, birds, insects and even seasonal human events. Even the type of rain that falls in a poem may have resonance in the emotions of the characters involved.

The same has been true of traditional attire. To be chic, one's kimono and *obi* patterns should be perfectly attuned to the occasion, the season and the time of day. The room where a formal tea ceremony is held should have just the right scroll hanging in the alcove and the right flower or blooming twig in the vase that greets the guests. And the confectionery that is served with the tea should reflect the season in color and shape.

While the Toshogu Grand Shrine may stand out as an example of highly ornate architecture, the stronger tendency in Japanese construction is to use natural, unpainted wood for various purposes. The plain wood of the buildings at the Grand Shrines in Ise, at one extreme, are left to weather naturally for twenty years before the buildings are rebuilt on an adjacent plot with new buildings using the same unpainted wood. Meanwhile, the more humble thatched-roofed farmhouses of the Shirakawa-go village are in similar fashion built with materials that are cut, bound and shaved but are not covered or hidden under any kind of coating. Even an ordinary residence in the city may have a tatami mat floor in one room or a ceiling covered with natural planking.

Awareness of seasonal change is not limited to the somewhat rarified world of traditional culture. It can also be detected in the foods that are served in Japanese-style restaurants. An astute guest recognizes the seasonality of the ingredients of a meal—whether it be fish, wild greens, mushrooms, or local vegetables—and the reason for the selection of a particular type of plate with a certain design and color that is perfect for that particular time of year. In the same way, the regular patrons of a Japanese confectionery will anticipate the arrival of a particular type of *wagashi* sweet when the plums bloom, when the rainy season arrives, when the autumn moon is full and when the new year comes.

The Japanese sensitivity to nature is partially due to the distinct seasons of the main island of Honshu from which sprang the fundamental elements of Japanese culture. While the archipelago stretches from Hokkaido with its frigid winters to Okinawa with its subtropical climate, the steady formation of Japan's traditions began and continued in Honshu and spread outward from the Nara-Kyoto region to Kamakura and on to Edo, current-day Tokyo.

Over time, the Japanese not only developed means of dealing with their local climate and weather but embracing it in their religious ceremonies, their agricultural rites and their celebrations. In winter, the people of Sapporo employ snow and ice to construct enormous fanciful castles, palaces, legendary heroes and historic scenes for everyone's enjoyment. Further south, the people of Yokote, in the central valley of Tohoku, pile up snow at the coldest time of year and make small *kamakura* for candles and large *kamakura* for children to sit in and cook a warm treat. Elsewhere, human visitors trek through the snow to watch macaques descend from their mountain habitat to soak contentedly in natural hot springs.

Spring brings first the plum blossoms then the cherry blossoms and every region of the country has riverbanks, mountain slopes, temples, shrines and boulevards where the flowers can be enjoyed.

Summer is a time for festivals to distract people from the heat. Tokyo's Sumida River, for example, becomes a venue for frequent fireworks displays that are among the best in the world. In the north, the people of Aomori fill the streets in the heat of August evenings to dance among lighted floats designed to look like legendary heroes.

When autumn comes, the leaves change color and people look to specific destinations where conditions will be just right on a particular day to see the yellow, orange and red leaves announce the arrival of the end of a natural cycle.

Whether you have visited Japan or are hoping to someday, the photographs in this volume include the anticipated and the unanticipated in each region. While it may not be possible to visit each of the nine regions of the country, it is hoped that the selected locations will give some indication of what they are like. Most visitors from abroad visit at least part of the Tokyo region and part of the Kyoto-Osaka region. With this in mind, the major destinations in each of these regions are presented together with the lesser-known destinations off the central transportation routes. But if time allows, the regions of the north and the south are highly accessible and they have considerable appeal. We hope this collection will encourage you to add an extra destination off the more frequently taken path.

James M. Vardaman
Ginza, Tokyo

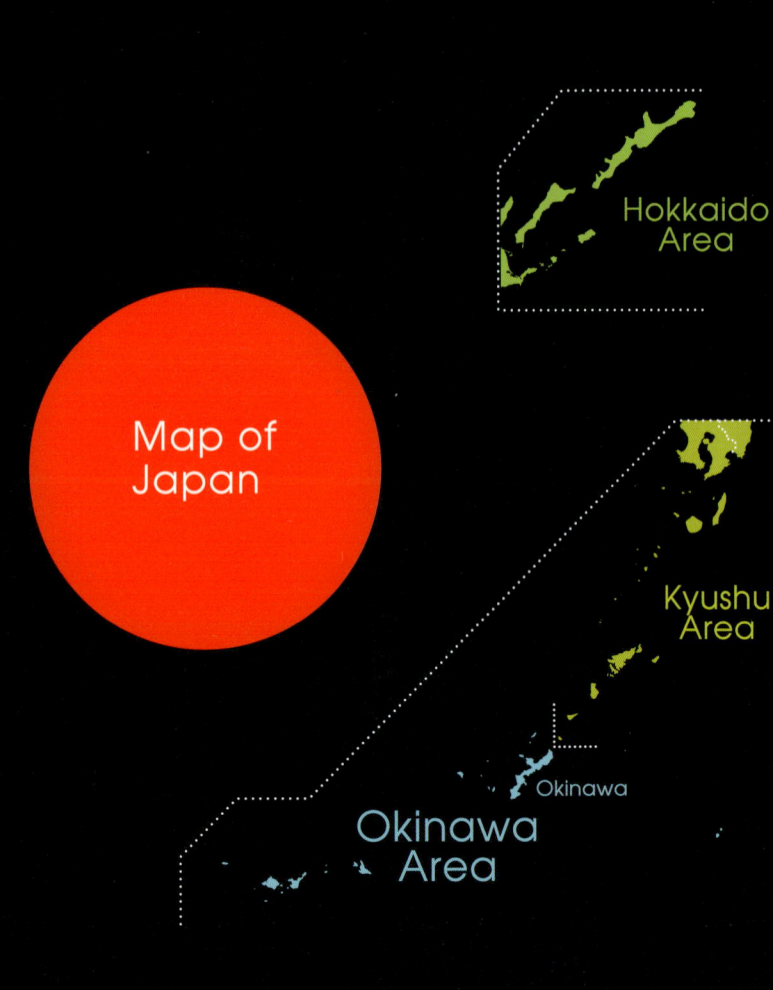

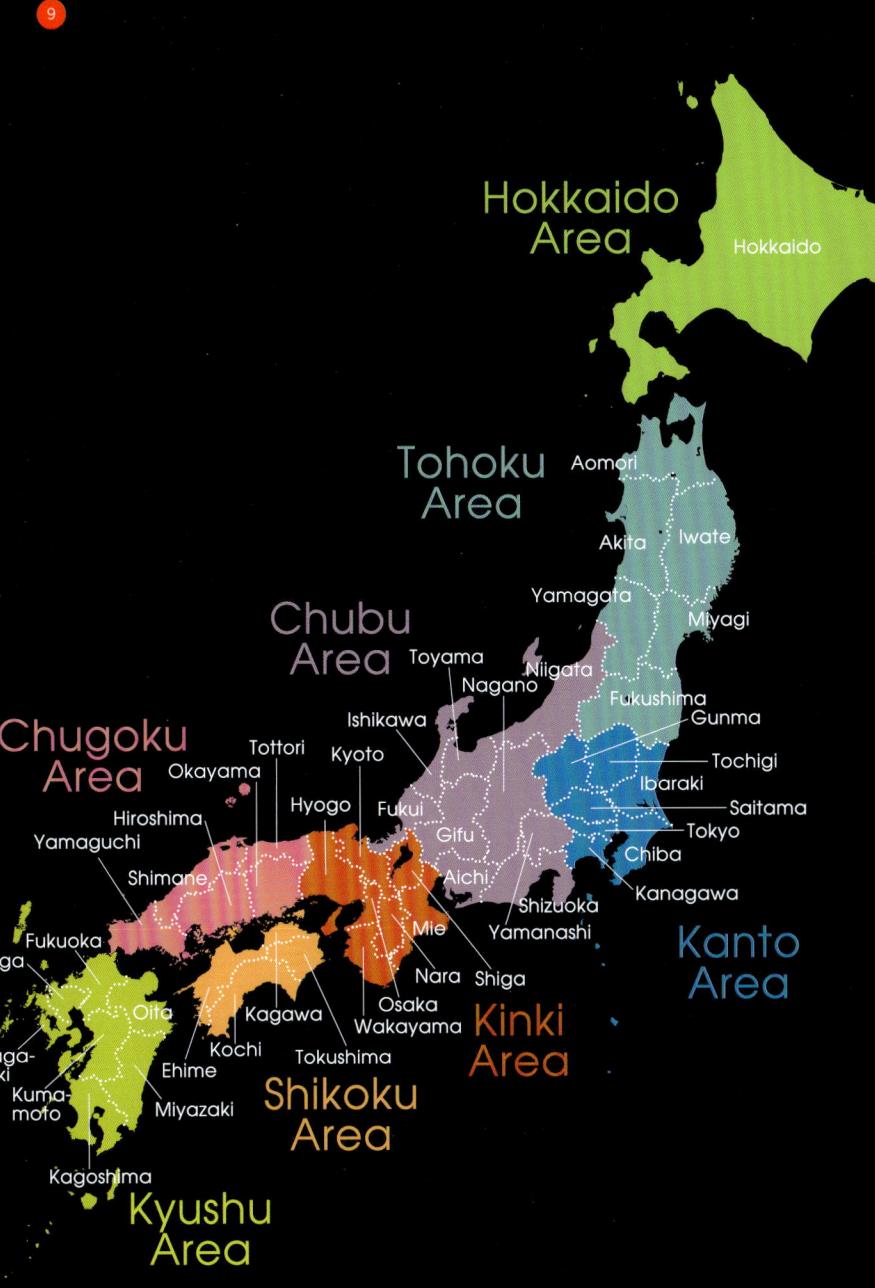

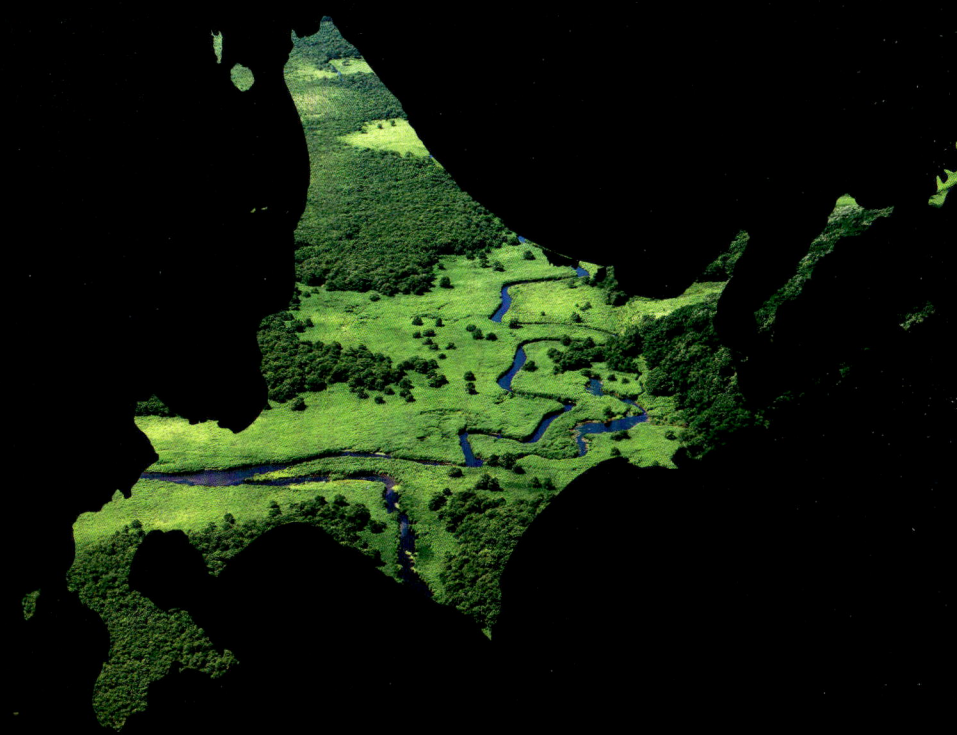

Hokkaido Area

The northernmost and second largest of Japan's main islands, Hokkaido is unlike the rest of the country in terms of climate, being considerably colder and drier. The land lies under snow during the frigid winters and plant life sprouts abundantly when the short summer warmth comes. Separated from Honshu by the Tsugaru Straits, the island was once occupied only by the Ainu people and was not considered a part of Japan. Beginning in the Edo period, Matsumae in the southwestern corner of the island was colonized, and in the Meiji period the new government began encouraging settlers from other parts of Japan to take up farming in the rich soil of the island. Significantly less populated than the rest of the country, Hokkaido offers a major change of pace to visitors from the other islands and absolutely spectacular scenery. Hakodate retains its distinctive historical heritage and a cityscape that draws tourists, while Sapporo serves as the island's political, economic and educational center. Hokkaido is known for its rugged central mountain range, broad hilly fields, crystal-clear lakes, marshlands and vast untouched forests, especially in the eastern Shiretoko Peninsula.

Hokkaido Area 12

Shiretoko Misaki Cape

The Shiretoko Peninsula in eastern Hokkaido has active volcanoes, waterfalls, lakes, coastal cliffs, and hot springs. Boats provide the best access to the peninsula's sights as roads are limited—and closed in winter—and wilderness trekking is not entirely advisable due to the high density of the brown bear population. Drift ice collects along the coast in winter carrying plankton that is consumed by small fish, including salmon and sea trout, which in turn attract bears and Steller's sea eagle, which has an enormous two-meter wingspan. The Shiretoko National Park is also home to Ezo deer, the Japanese red fox, and spotted seals.

Hokkaido Area

Sapporo Snow Festival

Held in February in the central Odori-koen Park, the Sapporo Snow Festival turns the monochrome snow and ice of winter into a colorful world of mythical figures, replicas of the wonders of the worlds, and animals, both real and imaginary. The event began in 1950 when local junior and senior high school students built six snow sculptures in the park. Year by year, the sculptures grew larger and now troops of the Self-Defense Force and groups of volunteers help by bringing in the equivalent of 6,000 dumptrucks' worth of snow for teams from around the world to work with. The festival also has elegant ice sculptures that are lit up at night.

Clock Tower, Sapporo

In the mid-nineteenth century when foreign fleets and merchants began making inroads in Japan, it was the Russians who first put their stamp on Hokkaido, leaving Russian Orthodox churches in some of its cities and the famous clock tower in Sapporo. The wooden building was originally part of Sapporo Agricultural School, present-day Hokkaido University. The clock tower has been the best-known symbol of Sapporo since 1878.

Otaru Canals

Once a thriving commercial and herring-fishing port on the coast west of Sapporo, Otaru sports several Western-style buildings from the booming times of the Meiji period. The most interesting of these are the stone and brick warehouses around the port, dating from the 1890s. Many have been restored and converted into cafes, coffee shops, art galleries, a glassworks and even a microbrewery. The Otaru canals, which was once filled with merchant barges, are now itself a major draw for visitors, especially when it is lit up in the evening.

Mikuni-toge Pass

Daisetsu-zan National Park is the largest national park in Japan. It consists of the Daisetsu-zan volcanic group whose highest peak is Asahidake at 2,291 meters above sea level. The park is known for its magnificent views, especially in the autumn when the foliage around the Soun-kyo Gorges, Lake Shikaribetsu, and the Ginga and Ryusei waterfalls turn a brilliant red. The highway passing over the Mikuni-toge Pass is the highest in Hokkaido.

Kushiro-shitsugen Marshland

Kushiro-shitsugen National Park is Japan's largest wetland, spreading over some 200 square kilometers. The wetlands are a bird sanctuary and winter season home of *tancho*, red-crowned cranes. The national bird, these graceful creatures grow to as much as 150 centimeters high. The white bird with a patch of red on its crown has long been a symbol of longevity, which is ironic given that Japan's modernization process almost drove it to extinction. In 1924 they were recognized

as a protected species and since then their populations in the Kushiro and Lake Akan areas have rebounded. As a result of an artificial breeding program initiated in the 1960s, the population has now risen dramatically. Photographers, kept at a safe distance, enjoy taking pictures of their elaborate mating dances.

Hokkaido Area 20

Traditional Ainu Dwelling

Ainu Lashed Boat

The indigenous inhabitants of Japan known today as Ainu were possibly related to ethnic groups that lived in Siberia. The Yamato people, who arrived in Japan via Kyushu and the Korean peninsula, gradually settled Honshu, causing the Ainu to retreat northward to Hokkaido. As the Yamato people began settling in Hakodate and other ports in Hokkaido, the Ainu began to assimilate rapidly, but since the 1980s attempts have been made to protect Ainu culture. This includes traditional clothing, dwellings, dugout canoes and religious rites.

Unkai Terrace

At 1,088 meters, the Unkai (Sea of Clouds) Terrace is not especially high, but the view of the ever-changing clouds from the observation deck from mid-May through mid-October can be stunning. A gondola reaches the terrace on the side of Mt. Tomamu where you can watch the clouds flow over the Hidaka Range, an especially impressive sight first thing in the morning.

Night View from Mt. Hakodate-yama

The port of Hakodate has flourished since 1741 when it became one of the first Japanese ports to open to foreign merchant ships under the treaties of the mid-1850s. It is a base for salmon, trout and squid fisheries as well as a market for Hokkaido's potatoes, rice and vegetables. Either shortly before dawn or at sunset, the view of the city and the Oshima Peninsula beyond from the top of the mountain is superb.

Goryo-kaku Fort at Hakodate

The Tokugawa Shogunate completed the Goryo-kaku Fort, named for its pentagonal star shape, in 1866 to defend Hakodate from foreign aggression. The Western-style citadel was the first of its kind in Japan. It is no small irony that the shogunate's troops made their last stand at this fort in 1869 when imperial forces defeated them in the fighting that solidified the Meiji Restoration.

Shirogane Blue Pond, Biei-cho

Not far from the colorful fields that make Furano a famous agricultural area is the small town of Biei-cho. The town is located in the hilly district at the foot of the Tokachi-dake Mountain Range and it became known primarily thanks to the landscape photographer Shinzo Maeda. The area is known for its magnificent views of colorful flowers such as lavenders, sunflowers, poppies, cosmoses, and purple salvias, blooming just like a beautiful patchwork, but the Shirogane Blue Pond has a mysterious appeal as well. It became famous when a certain computer company used its image as the wallpaper for a popular computer in 2012.

Lake Mashu-ko

A caldera lake in eastern Hokkaido, Lake Mashu-ko is the most transparent in Japan. The cliffs that surround it average 300 meters in height and in its center is Kamuishi Island, a lava dome. Although the lake has no inlet or outlet, the level of the water remains about the same year-round. The waters turn a deep, mysterious blue when they reflect the sunlight during the daytime. The fog that flows over the outer rim and covers the lake's entire surface makes for superb scenery.

Ice Floes

The bountiful environment of Shiretoko is in major part a gift from the Amur River, which spills into the Sea of Okhotsk and lowers the salt content of the seawater close to the surface. This water freezes in winter and drift ice, carrying plankton, forms ice floes that blanket the seas off of Shiretoko. When the ice melts, the plankton provide food for the food chain from small fish upward.

Lake Notoro, Abashiri Quasi-National Park

On the northeastern coast of Hokkaido facing the Sea of Okhotsk, the town of Abashiri is the gateway to some of the most beautiful natural wetlands and lakes in the country. One of the five lakes is Lake Notoro where, from spring to summer, local people gather at low tide to gather clams. In early autumn, the salt-marsh wetlands surrounding the lake turn into a red carpet of common glasswort. In winter, birdwatchers gather to see the swans, red-crowned cranes, and white-tailed sea eagles that gather in the area, while others come to ice-fish for smelt.

Furano

Located in the geographic center of Hokkaido, Furano's natural beauty is one part of the Furano-Ashibetsu Nature Park. In fall, the red and yellow tinted leaves are magnificent. In winter, one can enjoy the beautiful stardust in the sky. In spring, the charming flowers of *mizubasho*—skunk cabbage in English—appear along the roadsides. But it is the fields of fragrant lavender, tulips, daffodils and poppies in summer that draws the most attention.

Tohoku Area

Several mountain ranges divide the northern end of Honshu above the Kanto region from north to south. Like other regions, the Sea of Japan coast on the west has harsh winter weather and smaller populations, while the majority of cities are on the eastern Pacific Ocean coast. In addition there are cities in the central basin where rice agriculture is the main crop. A string of volcanoes, such as Mt. Osore, Mt. Iwate, Mt. Zao, and Mt. Bandai, are surrounded by hot springs that provide places to relax throughout the year. Summers are short in Tohoku and the people take advantage of that period to hold major festivals like Nebuta, Kanto and Tanabata. The winters are long and snowy, isolating some villages on occasion but also providing a large number of ski resorts. Agriculture tends toward rice in the limited flatlands with apples in the cooler northern areas. The area is seen as retaining more of the folk traditions, ways of thinking, close connectedness and endurance of earlier times.

Hirosaki Castle | AOMORI

Cherry trees bloom later in Hirosaki than in the Tokyo area and visitors hoping to see the blossoms head for the former site of Hirosaki Castle, one of the finest viewing spots in the Northeast. Even after the blossoms of the 5,000 trees fall, they form a beautiful raft of petals on the waters of the castle's moat. Hirosaki is also known for its bright lantern-lit floats, called *neputa*, which are pulled solemnly down the main streets in its early August festival. The Hirosaki floats are fan-shaped and their progress is announced by the thunderous beat of huge drums.

Nebuta Matsuri | AOMORI

Summer is short in Aomori and the local people know how to make the most of it. In August, the Aomori Nebuta festival unfolds around a raucous nighttime parade of huge bright-lit lantern floats decorated with famous figures from Japanese mythology and characters from Kabuki plays. The floats are wheeled through the city as *haneto* dancers energetically weave in and out between the floats, following the beat of massive drums that drive the participants to further enthusiasm.

Mt. Hakkoda | AOMORI

The Hakkoda Mountains, whose highest peak is the 1,585-meter Mt. O-dake, is a range of more than 17 lava domes and stratovolcanoes. These peaks slope gently into extensive marshlands. The mountains famously collect at least five meters of snow most winters and at higher elevations, the cold, wet wind turns the fir trees and conifers into "snow monsters", trees covered with frost that take on a unique appearance. Nearby Sukayu Onsen has been popular for its healing waters since the 17th century. The centerpiece is a "thousand-person" cypress bath, a public bath with mixed bathing, which measures 245 square meters.

Lake Towada and the Gorge of the Oirase River
| AOMORI and AKITA

Lake Towada fills a double volcanic crater in the Towada-Hachimantai National Park. Its crystal clear waters make it one of the most appealing natural attractions in northern Tohoku, especially in autumn when the leaves change color. Approaching the lake over the Hakka Pass, visitors have a superb view of the lake and the surrounding forests of beech and birch. After descending to lakeside, the casual walker can enjoy strolling along the shore at the village resort of Yasumiya. Most go to see a pair of bronze statues called *Maidens*, by well-known poet and sculptor Takamura Kotaro, which symbolize the dual craters joined by one lake.

At Nenokuchi where the lake spills into its only outlet, the Oirase River, which winds its way through moss-covered boulders and fallen trees to the village of Ishigedo.

Hotoke-ga-ura | AOMORI

The axe-shaped Shimokita Peninsula is the northernmost tip of Honshu, facing the Pacific Ocean to the east and the Tsugaru Strait to the west. A two-kilometer stretch of coastline on the peninsula at Hotoke-ga-ura has a group of peculiar-shaped pale rocks which are somehow reminiscent of images of Buddha (*hotoke*), thus the name "Buddha's beach." They were sculpted by the fierce gales and pounding waves that make the area a harsh environment.

Tachi-Neputa Matsuri | AOMORI

Brightly-lit standing lantern floats called *tachi-neputa* are the main attraction of the summer festival in Goshogawara, Aomori Prefecture. The colorful floats take the shape of some heroic character and some are 23 meters tall. A somewhat shorter version of one of these floats has also appeared in the Carnival parade in Sao Paulo, Brazil, to commemorate the 120th anniversary of diplomatic relations between the two countries.

Juniko | AOMORI

Japan's quasi-national parks are protected areas that include the northern Tohoku region of Tsugaru. The park here includes the remote Tsugaru Peninsula, the volcanic peaks of Mt. Iwaki, Cape Tappi and the two areas of wetlands and marshes called Juniko, literally "twelve lakes". Actually there are 33 lakes that were probably created by a landslide caused by an Edo period earthquake, but people could only see twelve from the collapsed mountain. The azure-blue Aoike is popular among hikers for the highly transparent waters, which reflect the colors of the leaves at its edge.

Kamakura, Yokote | AKITA

The small town of Yokote in the northern part of Akita Prefecture celebrates the cold winter weather in mid-February by making small igloo-like snow huts called *kamakura*. One type of *kamakura* is hand-sculpted by hand by schoolchildren on school grounds and along the riverbanks to provide shelter for a single candle. When the candles are lit in these 30-centimeter high mounds, their warm glow takes the edge off of the cold of the evening.

A larger type of *kamakura*, some three meters high and three and a half meters in diameter, is large enough to hold several children. Veteran *kamakura* builders construct more than 100 of these for children to enjoy. The children gather inside these temporary snow houses to enjoy grilled rice cake and amazake heated over a small charcoal grill.

Kiritanpo | AKITA

Tanpo is a long rice bar which is a specialty of Akita Prefecture. Cooked rice pounded until sticky is pressed onto cedar skewers which are then grilled over an open hearth. The rice can be eaten directly from the sticks as a snack. Home-cooking Akita-style calls for slicing off pieces of the roasted rice and adding it to a chicken-broth hotchpotch known around the country as "kiritanpo nabe." Each family has its own recipe and the dish is served on most special occasions.

Tohoku Area 38

Kakunodate | AKITA

Founded in 1620 by a local lord serving under the large Akita domain, this military outpost retains many historic samurai residences that have survived since the Edo period. They line the original wide avenues and their walls enclose gardens that befit the former military rulers of the town. The austere colors of the residences and surrounding walls serve as a stunning backdrop to the pale pink blossoms of the 400 some weeping cherry trees that come into bloom in spring. Not far from the samurai residences, cherry trees lining the bank of the Hinokinai River draw people from all over Tohoku during the cherry-blossom-viewing season.

Kanto Matsuri | AKITA

The major draw of Akita is the Kanto Festival held on August 3-6, during the consecutive, somewhat overlapping festivals across Tohoku. This is an impressive performance festival in which young men balance a 12-meter-long bamboo pole with 8 crossbars supporting 46 lighted paper lanterns. The 50-kilogram assembly is balanced in the palm of one hand, on the forehead, in the waistband and any other place that shows the holder's daring and skill.

Lake Tazawa-ko | AKITA

Lake Tazawa-ko at 423 meters is the deepest lake in the country. Almost perfectly circular, it is known for the peaks surrounding the lake being reflected in its crystal clear sapphire-blue waters. Pleasure boats and rowboats, swimmers and hikers make the lake a busy place during summer vacation, but in the other seasons the visitor can enjoy the scenery at leisure. On the western shore stands a golden statue of a legendary princess named Tatsuko, who was transformed into a dragon because she wished to possess eternal beauty. Be careful what you wish for.

Zenkoku Hanabi Kyogikai | AKITA

Pyrotechnicians from all over Japan gather in Omagari, Akita Prefecture, to display their skills in a national competition which has been held since 1910 and which many consider the top fireworks show in the country. About 10,000 large fireworks light up the night sky on the fourth Saturday of August each year.

Chuson-ji Temple, Golden Hall | IWATE

From the 11th through 12th centuries, the now isolated town of Hiraizumi was the home of three generations of Fujiwara lords who hoped to build an opulent, peaceful "northern capital" to compete with Kyoto. Built in 1124, the dazzling Konjikido, Golden Hall, covered in gold leaf, gilt plaques and gold-splashed lacquer is the masterpiece of the Chuson-ji Temple, which sits at the top of a slope lined with 300-year-old cryptomeria. The temple which haiku poet Basho referred to as "temple of light," honors Amida and is dedicated to those who fell in the wars of the Heian period.

A pond garden is all that remains of the 12th-century Motsu-ji, a monastery once populated by 500 priests. In early May, a procession of warriors in period costumes travels from Motsu-ji to Chuson-ji to honor the Fujiwara heyday. These two sites are registered as World Heritage Sites, but they were previously honored by Basho, who composed a haiku of great pathos when he visited and saw how the dreams of warriors ended in overgrown ruins of the magnificent dreams of a northern capital city.

Rikuchu Kaigan | IWATE

The Pacific Ocean incessantly batters the rugged 200-meter Kitayamazaki Cliffs on the Rikuchu Coast of Iwate Prefecture. In early summer, cold wet *yamase* winds from the mountains form a thick fog that shrouds the precipices creating a mystical seascape.

Wanko Soba | IWATE

Wanko soba is delicious buckwheat noodles served in little cups. Morioka is famous for turning this simple meal into a contest of how many small servings you can down at one sitting. A waitress stands behind you constantly replenishing your supply until you surrender. If you take on the challenge, you can choose to go over the average equivalent of 15 cups, the average for a man of about 50 cups or the amount your companion has consumed. The daily record in most restaurants is something over 140 servings.

Tohoku Area 44

Zao Okama and "Snow monsters" on Mt. Zao
| MIYAGI and YAMAGATA

Mt. Zao, on the border between Miyagi and Yamagata prefectures, attracts visitors through all seasons. In summer, Zao Okama, the caldera lake at the top which measures some 400 meters in diameter, attracts hikers. In the winter, the top of the mountain is covered with fantastic "snow monsters" or "snow ghosts" called *juhyo*. The phenomenon is caused by the wet, super-cold air that blows in from the Sea of Japan. When this air hits the fir trees at the top of the mountain, small water droplets instantaneously freeze on the trees, turning them into unique shapes.

Yamadera, Yamagata Prefecture | YAMAGATA

Founded in 860 by the Buddhist priest Ennin, Risshaku-ji Temple is popularly known as Yamadera. Just inside the entrance is Konpon Chudo, the temple where the sacred Flame of Belief has been burning constantly for a millennium with one minor interruption. The temple complex climbs up the side of a mountain overlooking fields and hills behind the small town of the same name. Visitors climb 1,015 steps to reach the sanctuary at the top for a superb view, especially during autumn.

Ginzan Onsen | YAMAGATA

Lining both sides of the Ginzan-gawa River, retro-modernized wooden inns from the Taisho and early Showa periods offer a traditional ambience with modern conveniences. The buildings of these inns are mostly three or four stories and they all share the milky white hot spring water that flows through the town with its several public bathhouses.

Tohoku Area 48

Hanami-yama Koen | FUKUSHIMA

Some sixty years ago a farmer in Fukushima decided to start planting cherry trees and other flowering trees on the slopes of the mountains around his farm. Each year he added planted more and his son continued the pattern until the present-day Hanami-yama Koen became a major attraction during April. Somei Yoshino cherry blossoms bloom together with peach trees, plums, magnolias, and camellias along the hills. The cherry blossoms usually bloom for only about a week after full-bloom. The small round petals of the cherry blossoms flutter to the ground in their final stage, symbolizing the beauty and transience of human life.

Ouchi-juku | FUKUSHIMA

During the Edo Period, the Tokugawa shogunate established a network of major roads and connecting roads throughout Honshu to enable the feudal lords and their retainers and servants to travel to Edo for service once every two years. At set distances along these post roads were places to eat and stay overnight. Along the Aizu Nishi Kaido route, connecting Nikko with Aizu-Wakamatsu, Ouchi-juku in present-day Fukushima prospered with the coming and going of these entourages. This village retains many of the old wooden houses with hipped thatch roofs, preserved as they were before the 1868 Meiji Restoration.

Tanabata Matsuri | MIYAGI

Sendai's Tanabata Matsuri, the Star Festival, is based on a Chinese legend of a weaver girl and her herder boyfriend, represented by the stars Vega and Altair, who fell in love and neglected their occupations. As punishment, the king of heaven placed them on opposite sides of the Milky Way and allowed them to meet only once a year, on the seventh day of the seventh month. In Sendai this is celebrated August 6-8 by hanging bamboo and paper streamers on bamboo poles in the main arcades. Visitors gather to admire the artistic creations and hope for a bit of breeze as a respite from the summer heat.

Naruko | MIYAGI

Naruko Gorge drops some 100 meters to the surface of the Otani-gawa River. On its sides, massive rocks have been shaped by wind and water to create natural works of art. In autumn the valley turns red and gold, contrasting strikingly with the white bridge that spans the gorge. At Naruko Onsen, the Onsen-jinja Shrine enshrines the hot spring waters that first gushed out in 837 when the Naruko Volcano erupted. The Takinoyu public bathhouse draws water straight from the shrine's spring source, filling the bath with milky blue-white water.

Mt. Osore-zan | AOMORI

Mt. Osore-zan was once a training ground for Buddhist monks. The name literally means "terrible mountain" and it is not hard to understand why. The harsh winds, sulfur fumes from the dead lake that fills part of the caldera, and the desolate yellow and red-stained landscape alone are unworldly. Among the local people, the mountain has long been held to be a place where the worlds of life and death connect. Not too far from the shore of nearby Lake Usori is a temple dedicated to the spirits of children who have died. Visitors leave colored pinwheels in memory of the departed souls and add to piles of rocks scattered along the shore as a symbolic way of helping those who are suffering in the Buddhist netherworld.

Kanto Area

The Kanto region in east central Honshu is the most heavily populated area of the country and its political, economic and cultural center. The regional center is the metropolitan area consisting of Tokyo, Yokohama, Kawasaki and Chiba, an almost continuous urban area. The city of Edo was not founded until 1604, when the Tokugawa shogunate made it the center of military power. In 1868, Edo became Tokyo, "Eastern Capital," and with the move of the Emperor to the palace at the city's heart, the centripetal forces of the city made it the center of the country. The Kanto Plain occupies more than half of the region. Half of the plain is volcanic ash and the other half is primarily river deltas of the Tonegawa, Arakawa, and Tamagawa rivers.

While the megapolis is a source of newer cultural forms, cultural heritage in Nikko and Kamakura hark back to the Edo period and even earlier. On the periphery of the great Kanto Plain, natural areas such as the Ozegahara marshland provide a different perspective of the region. Even more stunning are the Izu Islands and the Ogasawara Islands that stretch south of the region into the Pacific.

Nikko Toshogu | TOCHIGI

A sacred mountain for ascetics beginning in the Nara period, Nikko is the site of *Toshogu*, the mausoleum of Tokugawa Ieyasu, the founder of the Tokugawa shogunate. His grandson Iemitsu built the elegantly decorated shrine to symbolize the long-lasting peace that Ieyasu created. It is now a major attraction.

Sleeping Cat | TOCHIGI

Toshogu mixes Shinto with Buddhism. The main hall is a Shinto shrine. The pagoda is Buddhist. There is a Buddhist sutra storehouse. The chief figure in the construction of Toshogu was a Buddhist monk named Tenkai, but he chose to make Ieyasu a Shinto god instead of a Buddha.

Three Wise Monkeys | TOCHIGI

At the approach to the shrine gate is a stable for sacred horses. One of the panels under the roof is one with three monkeys (*sanzaru*) that teaches that gem of wisdom "see no evil, hear no evil, speak no evil." The *Yomei-mon* gate is elaborately carved and multicolored. Inside is another gate called *Kara-mon*. It is only open on special occasions, such as when state guests visit. The main shrine is an important space where the worlds of gods and humans connect.

Kegon-no-taki Waterfall | TOCHIGI

A visit to the Tokugawa mausoleum or Toshogu is often paired with a visit to Lake Chuzenji-ko on the mountain above the shrine. The lake was created when Mt. Nantai-san erupted and blocked off a river. Water from the lake now has its only outlet in the impressive Kegon-no-taki Waterfall,

Odashiro-ga-hara | TOCHIGI

West of Nikko, location of the magnificent Toshogu Shrine, is a wetland area registered as a protected site under the Ramsar Convention. At an elevation of 1,000 meters, the area is cool during the summer months and therefore attracts visitors eager to escape the heat of the lowlands. In addition to Lake Chuzenji-ko, Oku-Nikko, as the area is called, includes Senjo-ga-hara and Odashiro-ga-hara. The latter is a small marshland located west of the Yukawa River that is surrounded by a beech forest.

considered one of the three most beautiful falls in Japan. The water drops straight down from a 97-meter-high cliff, raising plumes of mist at the basin, which is particularly impressive after a heavy rain. Twelve smaller falls leak through cracks midway down the mountainside. The falls freeze in winter, creating a cascade of icicles.

Oarai-kaigan Coast | IBARAKI

Among popular tourist destinations for young people are places that appear in anime and manga. Oarai in Ibaraki Prefecture is one of those "sacred spots" due to a unique animated story of a group of girls who operate tanks. Featured in the series is a *tonkatsu* restaurant and a hotel that actually exist. For non-fans, the Kamiiso no Torii gate at Oarai Isosaki-jinja Shrine is the site of particularly beautiful sunrises.

Fukurodano-taki Falls | IBARAKI

Located on the Kuji-gawa River, the Fukurodano-taki Falls are among the most impressive waterfalls in the country, especially during the autumn when the foliage is changing. In winter, the falls freeze, which draws a sturdier type of sightseer. The Heian poet Saigyo and the lord of the Mito domain Tokugawa Mitsukuni are among those who visited the four-stage falls and composed poems commemorating their beauty.

Kusatsu Onsen | GUNMA

In northwestern Gunma Prefecture, the town of Kusatsu has been famous since the 12th century for its hot springs. It is located in the foothills of Mt. Shirane-san, an active volcano in the Nasu Volcanic Zone. The hot springs at Kusatsu are known for their sulfur and iron content and for their high temperature of 60 degrees Celsius. To cool the water at least slightly, it is allowed to flow across seven long wooden boxes called *yu-batake*, "hot-spring fields", in the center of the resort before passing on to 130 some inns in the village. At night the beautifully lit cooling troughs are an impressive sight.

Ozegahara Marshland | GUNMA

Two kilometers long and six kilometers wide, Ozegahara is the largest highland marshland in the country at some 1,400 meters above sea level. In spring when the snow begins to melt, the basin is filled with *mizubasho*, skunk cabbage, which bloom all at one time. In summer, bright yellow *kisuge* lilies cover the landscape. In autumn the area turns yellow, orange and bright red. The marshland can be traversed via elevated boardwalks and is very popular among hikers.

Tomioka Silk Mill Site | GUNMA

During the late 1800s, the Tomioka Silk Mill in Gunma Prefecture became the center of an industry that spread throughout the surrounding area. Sericulture centered on the cultivation of mulberry trees, the leaves of which were used to feed the silkworms which produced the cocoons that were turned into silk thread and were then transported to the mill. The government imported French silk-reeling technology to raise the quality of silk production. The Tomioka Silk Mill, built in 1872, is the centerpiece of a large cultural landscape, which contributed to making Japan the largest exporter of raw silk in the world by 1909.

Kanto Area 62

Sawara | CHIBA

In the small town of Sawara, especially in the *suigo* district with its many waterways, the streets remain much as they were in the Edo period, some two hundred years ago. Merchants prospered from trade along the river connecting the north with Edo, and built homes along a section of the Onogawa River, a tributary of the major Tonegawa River transportation route. The area is now a national preservation district due to its group of historic buildings. Some are warehouse-style (*kurazukuri*) houses and many are family businesses that have survived to the present day. Excursion boats along the river provide a unique view of the town.

Kawagoe | SAITAMA

A small castle town which the Tokugawa shogunate valued because it protected the northern approach to Edo, Kawagoe suffered major damage in a fire in 1893. That fire encouraged the local merchants to build a fire-watch bell tower, now the symbol of the town, and construct fire-resistant clay-plastered *kurazukuri*, warehouse-style combinations of residence and business, many of which are still standing. Some are now museums, but shops selling local hand-made candy, chic traditional accessories, and local draft beer made from sweet potato make the one-hour trip to Hon-Kawagoe Station from Shinjuku an enjoyable daytrip.

Chiba Isumi Railroad | CHIBA

Central Chiba Prefecture is traversed by the Isumi and Kominato railways, which pass through beautiful stretches of wildflowers, cultivated flowers, rugged valleys and hot springs. The Yoro Valley Hot Spring along this rail route offers superb views during the warmer seasons and the autumn changing of the colors. The Awamata-no-taki Waterfall is especially known for its clear waters which drop gradually over a distance like a piece of silk spread over the surface.

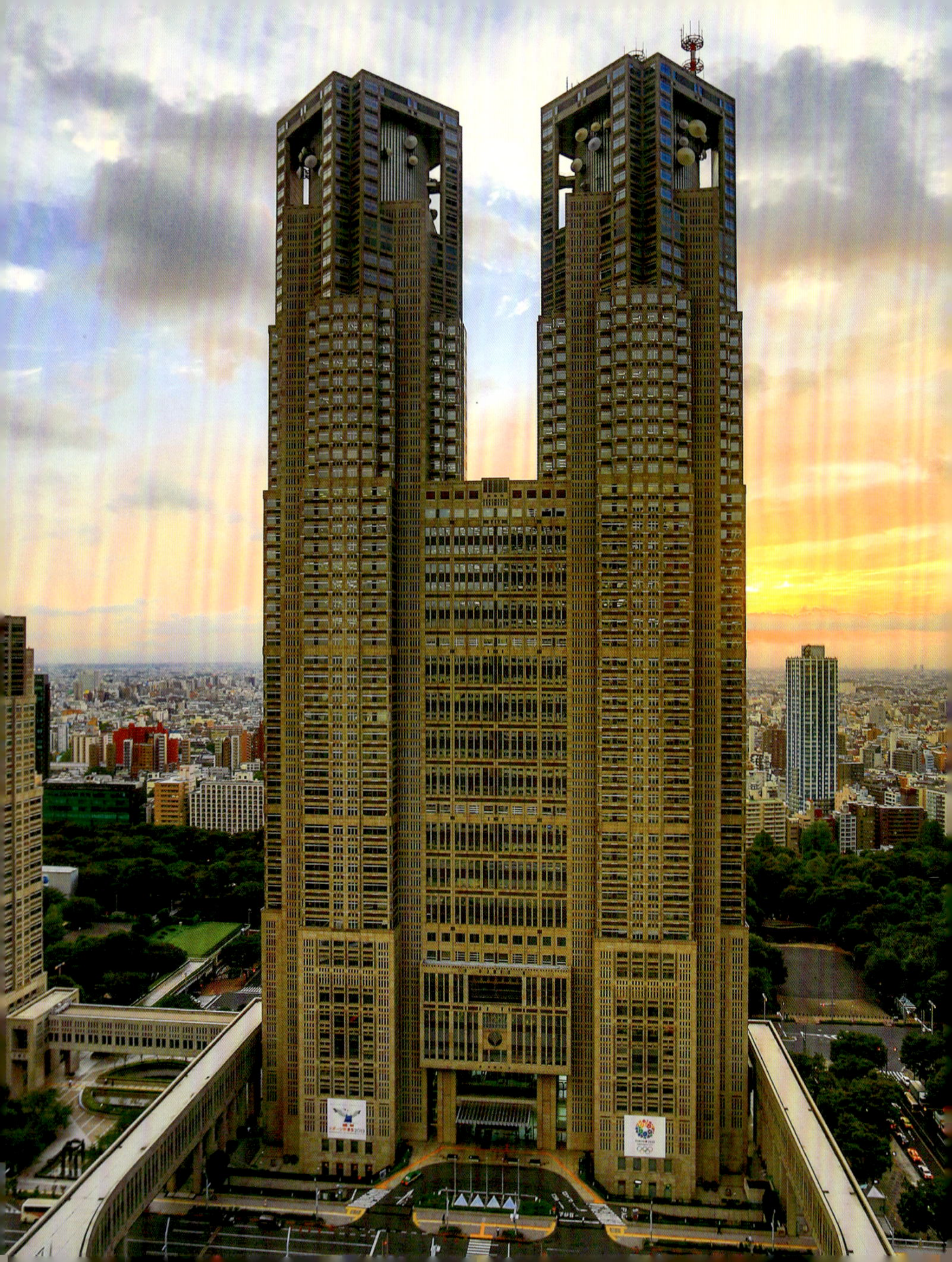

Shinjuku District, Tokyo Metropolitan Government Office Building | TOKYO

Shinjuku Station is the gateway to the western parts of the Tokyo metropolis via three subways and seven commuter railway lines. The east side of the station is a concentration of shops, department stores, restaurants, boisterous Kabuki-cho, and Shinjuku Gyo-en National Garden. The west side has upscale hotels, more department stores but is characterized more by tall buildings and the Tokyo Metropolitan Government Office complex. Observation decks on the 45th floors of both towers of the metropolitan headquarters are free and offer the best view of Mt. Fuji from the center of the city.

Tokyo Station | TOKYO

Tokyo Station opened as the hub of the capital city in 1914, a red-brick building facing the Imperial Palace on the Marunouchi side. The building was destroyed in the air raids of World War II and rebuilt following the war, but it was not restored to its original plan until 2012. The restored building has the octagonal domed roofs, a chic hotel, and a special entrance reserved for the Imperial Family. Illuminated in the evening, this side of the station is a favorite spot for photographers. The opposite side is called the Yaesu exit and it too has recently completed major renovations.

The National Diet Building | TOKYO

The National Diet Building is in Nagata-cho, Chiyoda Ward, just across from the Imperial Palace. The 65-meter tall pyramid-like granite tower in the center is flanked by the House of Representatives in the left wing and the House of Councilors in the right wing. It was complete in 1936 and was the tallest building in Japan at that time. Following the centennial of the establishment of the Diet in 1990, the Diet Building has been lit up every evening.

Tokyo Tower | TOKYO

When Tokyo Tower was completed in 1958 in the Roppongi area, at 333 meters it became a symbol of Tokyo, the major broadcast antenna for the Tokyo region, and a favorite sightseeing destination. Modeled on the Eiffel Tower, it was purposely built 13 meters taller to outdo the Paris masterpiece. From the observation decks at 150 meters and 250 meters, one can still get good views of the city, including Mt. Fuji to the west. The way it is illuminated at night depends on the season and special events that are being held in the city.

Tokyo Skytree | TOKYO

Tokyo Tower was once the main broadcasting tower in Tokyo, but in 2012, it was replaced by the multipurpose 634-meter Tokyo Skytree in Sumida Ward, recognized by the Guinness World Records Company as the tallest free-standing tower in the world. It serves as a digital terrestrial broadcasting tower, and has observation decks at 350 meters and 450 meters, each with a 360-degree panoramic view. The tower is illuminated with LEDs in various ways, including sky-blue *iki* (chic) patterns and purple *miyabi* (elegant) patterns.

Senso-ji, Asakusa | TOKYO

The oldest temple in Tokyo, Senso-ji dates from 628, when two fishermen found a small gold image of the Kannon Bodhisattva in their fishing net. The local people built a small temple for the statue near the Sumida River. Since that time, the temple has been destroyed and rebuilt many times.

Sanja Festival | TOKYO

One weekend in May, the Asakusa district hosts the annual Sanja Festival, a celebration of the three founders of the Senso-ji Temple. During the three days of the festival, some two million people visit Asakusa, making it one of the three largest festivals in the Tokyo area. One hundred portable shrines parade through the streets to bring good fortune to the businesses and residents. On the final Sunday, three large portable shrines from the Asakusa Shrine itself appear. Drums and flutes provide music for dancers and food stalls and festival games entertain in other ways.

The main gate of the temple houses the God of Wind and the God of Thunder, who are believed to protect against fire and natural disasters and bring large harvests. The gate is called *Kaminari-mon*, literally "Thunder Gate", and is famous for its enormous red paper lantern. Between this gate and the temple is a long arcade called Nakamise-dori. Shops along both sides sell souvenirs of varying quality, *senbei* (rice crackers), traditional sweets, woodblock prints, *tenugui* (printed towels) and miniature figures based on traditional themes.

Nihonbashi Bridge | TOKYO

From the time the first wooden bridge was constructed, the Nihonbashi Bridge has been commemorated in wood-block prints and photographs as the starting point of all of the major highways of Japan. All the distances of those roads were calculated from its center. In 1962, however, the bridge was held in such low esteem that, in preparation for the 1964 Olympics, an expressway was built right above it. Fans of the bridge with its famous lion sculptures, however, hope that one day it will be exposed to the sunlight once more.

Ginza | TOKYO

Ginza, literally "silver mint", was the location of mints for casting silver coins in the early 17th century by the Tokugawa shogunate. In the early Meiji period, it became a center of Western fashion and culture. Following a fire that destroyed most of the area in 1872, the government designated Ginza as an area for the construction of fireproof brick structures. Today Ginza is one of the most upscale shopping districts in the world. Its center is Ginza-dori, which is closed to vehicular traffic on weekends and holidays. Both sides of the street are lined with department stores and expensive boutiques. Along the back streets are art galleries, coffee shops, restaurants and bars.

Kabukiza Theater | TOKYO

The Kabukiza Theater was built in 1889 as a special theater for traditional Kabuki performances. Since then it has undergone several restorations, the most recent of which was completed in April 2013. While the new facility has a 29-story office building at the rear, the façade of the theater itself retains the characteristic Momoyama-style architecture, including a gabled tiled roof and Japanese-style balustrades.

Imperial Palace | TOKYO

The Imperial Palace occupies the grounds of the former Edo Castle. It is possible to stroll through the Imperial Palace East Garden in which there is one of the original watchtowers. On the opposite side of the palace, the Chidori-ga-fuchi National Memorial Garden on the moat is one of the best places in the city to view cherry blossoms. There is no regular access to the palace grounds, with the exception of two days when the Emperor and his family greet well-wishers at the New Year and on his birthday. On those days, visitors pass over the elegant, double-arched Niju-bashi Bridge.

Meiji-jingu Shrine | TOKYO

In the middle of the city and just across the railway line from the heart of the Omotesando fashion district, Meiji-jingu Shrine is dedicated to the spirit of the Emperor Meiji (1852-1912) during whose reign Japan's rapid modernization took place. The shrine is set off by a huge *torii* gate and is surrounded by a forest of trees gathered from around the country. The shrine is Tokyo's largest draw at New Years, with some one million coming to pray for health, wealth and whatever else in the coming year.

The shrine is surrounded by a large impressive wooded park and it has several types of gardens as well. One is the Iris Garden which has some 150 varieties of irises which begin to bloom in mid-June and are in full bloom for about two weeks. Next to the shrine grounds is the separate Yoyogi Park, where many people come to picnic on weekends.

Shibuya Scramble Crossing | TOKYO

On the north side of JR Shibuya Station are two Tokyo landmarks. One is the statue of Hachiko, the faithful dog who went to meet his master at the train station every evening, and continued to do so even after his master passed away. The statue is a popular place for people to meet. The second is the scramble crossing, where crowds of people from four corners wait for the red lights to stop all traffic and allow a mass of humanity to flow across. Stimulated by the movie "Lost in Translation", visitors from abroad seem to find this a fascinating experience, especially at rush hour.

Shinjuku Kabuki-cho | TOKYO

Some 3.64 million people pass through the complex Shinjuku Station, composed of JR, private railways, and subways, on an average day. Some of those people drawn by the neon lights end up in Kabuki-cho, to the east of the station, which is a major cluster of bars, night clubs, casual izakaya and other forms of entertainment.

Odaiba | TOKYO

A *daiba* is a battery or fort, but *Odaiba* is a popular leisure zone of arcades, shopping malls, museums, apartment buildings, hotels, a sand beach and a Ferris wheel. The huge complex built on landfill in Tokyo Bay is connected to Shinbashi Station by the Yurikamome Monorail.

Kamakura Great Buddha
| KANAGAWA

The casting of this bronze image of Amitabha Buddha, weighing 125 tons, began in 1252, but it is not clear when it was actually completed. It is 11.3 meters high and was, despite its current bluish-green appearance, once covered in gold leaf. It now stands in the open, but was originally housed in a great hall like the bronze statue of the Buddha Vairocano at Todai-ji in Nara. The structure was lost in 1495, but it is not clear whether it was destroyed by fire, earthquake, typhoon or tsunami. The statue is hollow and visitors can go inside.

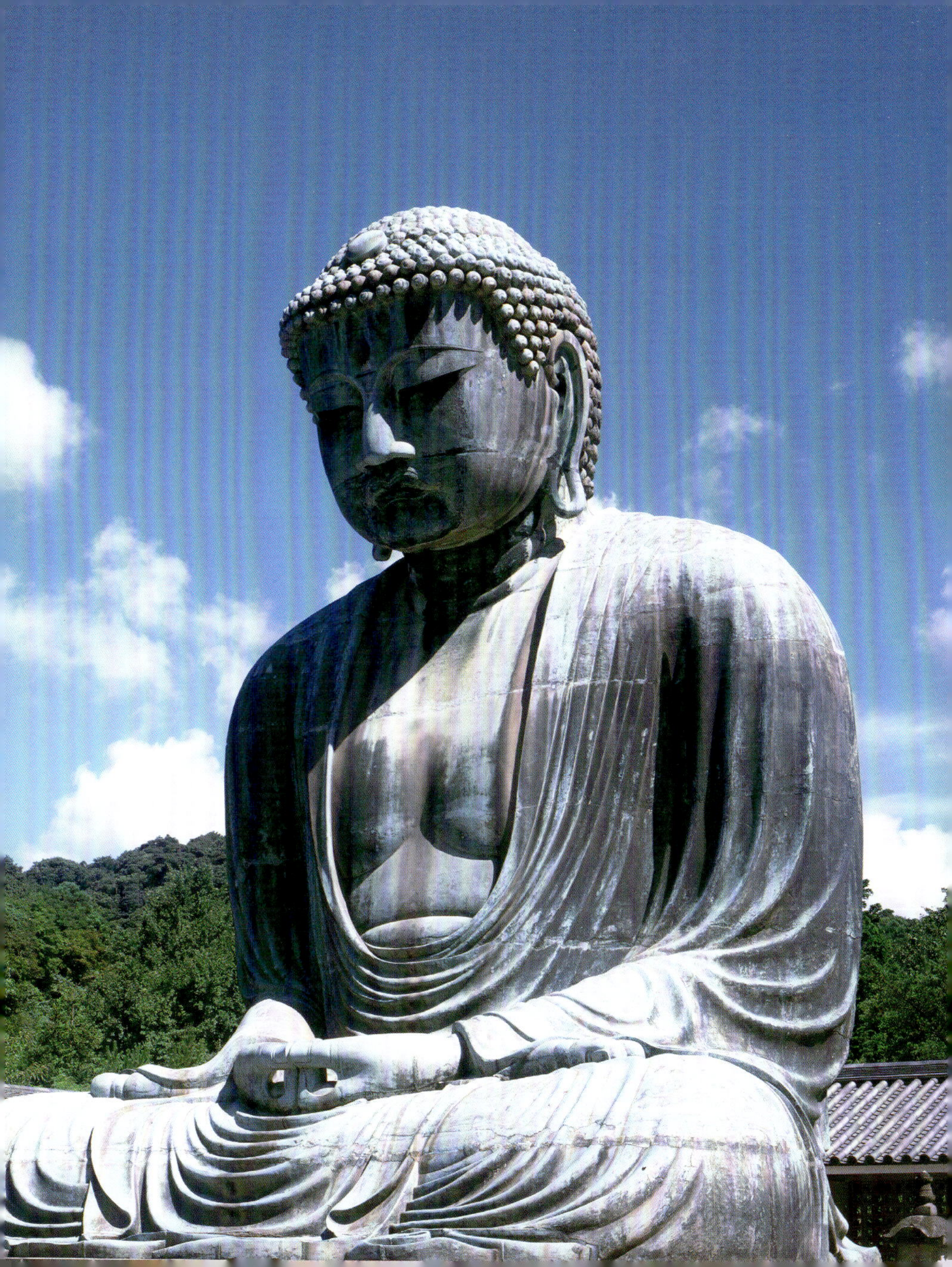

Minato Mirai, Yokohama | KANAGAWA

The Minato Mirai 21 complex was built on reclaimed land just outside Sakuragi-cho Station in the harbor at Yokohama. The Landmark Tower is an impressive 296 meters tall and has one of the world's fastest elevators at 45 km/h. The lower floors are devoted to shops and restaurants, but the 69th floor observatory is a great place to view Mt. Fuji and Tokyo Bay. The Yokohama Museum of Art, behind Landmark Tower, exhibits both European classical artwork and modern Japanese artists.

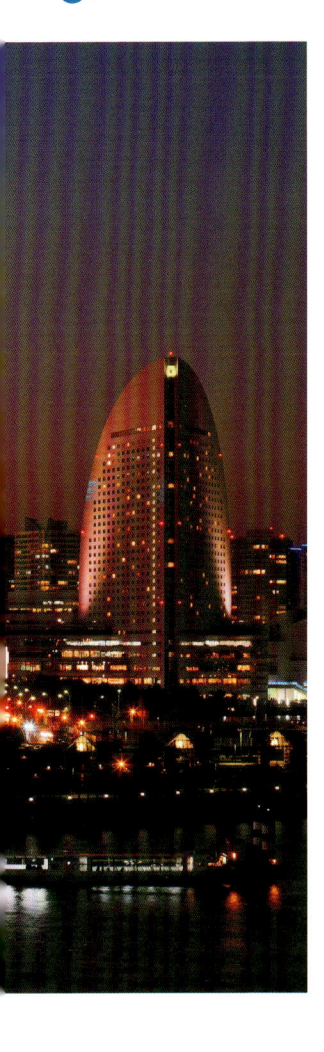

Yokohama Chinatown | KANAGAWA
The elaborate Goodwill Gate marks the entrance to the largest Chinatown in Japan. This distinctive large Chinese settlement has more than 350 shops selling foodstuffs, herbal medicine, cookware and toys, in addition to 160 restaurants serve every variety of Chinese cuisine. Immigrants from Shanghai and Hong Kong came to live when the port of Yokohama opened at the end of the Edo period. It is now the top tourist destination in Yokohama.

Lake Ashi-no-ko | KANAGAWA

Lake Ashi-no-ko in the resort area of Hakone provides close-up views of Mt. Fuji. On the shore is the town of Hakone, which at one time was on the Tokaido, the main highway that connected the imperial capital at Kyoto with the shogunate headquarters at Edo. The Hakone Barrier, a checkpoint that monitored people coming from and going to Edo, present-day Tokyo, was a key means of maintaining political and military control over the country. A reconstruction of the checkpoint now serves as a small museum.

Hakone Tozan Tetsudo | KANAGAWA

This route over the mountains from Odawara up to the Gora, on the way to Hakone-Yumoto, takes a leisurely 54 minutes to travel 16 kilometers. It uses three switchbacks to slowly climb the steep grade, but the views are spectacular the higher the train climbs. From Gora, a cable car reaches Mt. Soun-zan.

Ogasawara Islands | TOKYO

The Ogasawara Islands are governed by the Tokyo Metropolitan Government, but they are more than a thousand kilometers south of Tokyo. These 30-some islands were uninhabited until the 1830s and were first settled by people from the Pacific Islands and the West. Chichi-jima and Haha-jima, literally "Father Island" and "Mother Island", are the only two islands currently inhabited, and they are popular departure points for divers and nature lovers. Ferries reach several of the islands once a week—if the weather cooperates. The islands are known as a breeding ground for humpback whales and as a good place to watch dolphins and green turtles.

Chubu Area

This scenic central region of Honshu is largely mountainous, dominated by the Japanese Alps and volcanoes including Mt. Fuji. The region is divided into three districts: the Tokai region facing the Pacific Ocean, the snowy Hokuriku region facing the Sea of Japan and the Central Highlands with mountain ranges over 3,000 meters high. On the north side, the Niigata Plain is one of the largest rice-producing parts of the country and Niigata is the largest city on the Sea of Japan coast. Nagoya, the largest city in the Chubu region, is the political, financial and cultural center of the Pacific coastal area between Tokyo and Osaka. Its castle is a major tourist attraction. Between these two urban centers, the cities of Takayama and Kanazawa and the post towns that lined the ancient roads connecting Kyoto and Edo retain the atmosphere of several centuries ago. Elsewhere in the countryside, the *gassho-zukuri* village of Shirakawa-go maintains a traditional agricultural heritage.

Kenrokuen Garden | ISHIKAWA

Kanazawa's masterpiece of Edo period landscape gardening takes the name *kenroku* from a famous Chinese garden which supposedly possessed the six qualities of perfect horticulture. The garden was originally part of a villa in Kanazawa Castle. The garden is especially beautiful through the warm months, but it is also an attraction even in winter, when the branches of the trees are suspended from ropes attached to the top of a post set at the center of the tree. Designed to protect the branches from breaking under heavy snowfalls, the elegant conical shapes show just how much care has gone into keeping this garden intact since it was conceived.

Shiroyone Rice Terraces | ISHIKAWA

Noto Peninsula, which hooks out into the Sea of Japan, is one of the better places to enjoy yellowtail and crab in the winter months and oysters and abalones in the summer. The masterpiece of the landscape is surely the breathtaking rice terraces on the cliffside at Shiroyone. These beautiful, varied-sized terraced rice paddies are the result of generations of dedicated farmers making full use of the limited land they have. The well-tended fields are undoubtedly part of the reason the region has been recognized as a Globally Important Agricultural Heritage System.

Kanazawa | ISHIKAWA

Few cities have the mixture of rich Edo period culture and sophisticated 21st-century culture that Kanazawa possesses. With the opening of a new Shinkansen line, the city has become an even more popular destination. The Kenroku-en Garden, begun in 1676 and completed in the early 1880s, is the masterpiece of the city, but its former samurai quarters in Nagamachi and the temple cluster in Teramachi make this city a deeply fascinating place. Myoryu-ji Temple, known also as Ninja-dera, where martial-arts masters once trained, only adds to its image as a once-powerful feudal domain.

Higashi-chaya | ISHIKAWA

Kanazawa as a whole retains the feel of the Edo period. Lying at the foot of the temple-covered Utatsuyama, Higashi-chaya Street is an exceptionally attractive area of that city with classical wooden architecture that dates back well over a century. The *chaya* were entertainment houses to which geisha were once called to perform for wealthy patrons.

Tarai-bune | NIIGATA

Wooden tub-like oval boats called *tarai-bune* were once used for fishing by the women of the small town of Ogi on Sado Island. Navigating with a single oar and using a glass-bottomed bucket to get a clear view of what is on the bottom in coves along the coast, fisherwomen used a long pole to snag abalone (*awabi*), wreath shells (*sazae*) and seaweed.

Yamakoshi | NIIGATA

Yamakoshi-mura was an ordinary mountain village until a well-known Japanese ethnologist helped promote the fact that it maintained long-held traditions to the present day. The village drew attention to its mountainside forests, its terrace fields, the cultivation of brocade carp and a local form of bullfighting, in which two bulls compete to make the other one back off. The village was also became the location for the filming of an NHK morning drama series called "Kokoro". The village suffered severe damage in an earthquake in 2004.

Tojinbo | FUKUI

Along the Japan Sea coast northwest of Fukui are towering rock formations with a legendary past. According to one version, villagers in 1182 threw an evil priest named Tojinbo from to the top of the cliffs, resulting in churning seas for the 49 days that followed. The villagers attributed the phenomenon to the wrath of the priest seeking revenge for his untimely death.

Eihei-ji | FUKUI

One of the most influential Zen temples in Japan, this training site was purposely established by Dogen, founder of the Soto Sect, far away from the capital at Kyoto in 1244. The cedar-lined stone stairs leading up the Chokushi-mon Gate is reserved for imperial envoys, but the other gates allow you into the complex, where you can observe some 200 resident monks going about their daily duties.

Ichijodani Asakurashi Iseki | FUKUI

The Asakura Family Historic Site in the Ichijo-dani Valley was the home of the family that governed the Echizen region of what is now Fukui Prefecure. The family controlled the area during the Warring States Period in the late 16th century, but when Oda Nobunaga began his conquest of the whole country, the Asakura residence was burned to the ground. All that remains are a gate, mounds and ditches that indicate the basic layout of the mansion and its gardens.

Kamikochi | NAGANO

The narrow Kamikochi valley in the Japan Alps within Chubu Sangaku National Park lies between several serious peaks. The valley itself is roughly 1,500 meters above sea level, making it a cool retreat in the summer and a favorite place to see the changing foliage early in the autumn. From the valley trails lead to Hotaka-dake, at 3,190 meters the third highest peak in Japan, and Yari-ga-take, named for its sharp spear-like peak.

Shiraito-no-taki, Karuizawa | NAGANO

Karuizawa is the oldest upland resort town in Japan and a century ago the older part, which forms Karuizawa Heights, became the summer residence of many foreign and national dignitaries, who sought relief from the heat in the Kanto area. A particularly refreshing sight in summer and a colorful sight in autumn is a local waterfall. What Shiraito Falls lacks in dynamism, it makes up for in elegance. The falls are only three meters high but spread out over some 70 meters in breadth, and its slender streaks appear like white threads trickling into the pond below.

Matsumoto Castle | NAGANO

Known as "Crow Castle" because it is painted black, this five-story castle is unusual for being connected to a smaller three-storied keep and another two-storied yagura. No other castle in Japan has this complex structure. The tallest stronghold is the oldest surviving tower of its type in Japan, due in no small part to the fact that no battles ever took place here. In spring, from the top of the castle one can see the remaining snow on the upper reaches of the Japan Alps beyond the cherry blossoms within the grounds of the castle.

Mt. Fuji and Shinkansen | NAGANO

The beautiful slopes of Mt. Fuji were created by smooth flows of lava from the caldera at the top. The most recent eruption of this active volcano was in 1707. Because there are no other mountains nearby to block the view, its slopes are clearly visible especially in winter, from many high points in central Tokyo.

Chubu Area

Tenku no Sato, Iida, | NAGANO

Near the city of Iida in Nagano Prefecture, a section of land between 800 and 1000 meters above sea level has become a popular destination due to its designation as one of the best villages in the country, its steep location (as much as 38 degrees) and its serving as a model for a Studio Ghibli animated film. The local people have built an observation point called *Tenku no sato*, "village in the skies", looking out over the valley.

Nihon kamoshika | NAGANO

The Japanese serow, or *kamoshika*, is a goat-antelope that lives in dense forests primarily in northern part of Honshu. It is found only in Japan. The adult reaches 80 some centimeters and weighs between 30 and 45 kilograms. Its bushy fur is black to whitish. Serows are solitary in nature and gather in small groups to eat herbs, leaves, acorns and bamboo shoots. In the mid-20th century, the serow was virtually hunted to extinction, but the government passed a law to protect it, and its populations have rebounded.

Jigokudani-yaen Koen | NAGANO

The denizens of Jigokudani Monkey Park are wild macaques who freely come and go between the mountains and the fence-less park that they rule. In winter the monkeys sleep in the hills nearby and descend during the day to eat the food that is provided and to warm themselves in the waters of a natural hot spring, much to the amusement of photographers who tread through the snows to the hot spring to observe them.

Shirakawa-go Village | GIFU

Central Japan has one of the heaviest snowfalls in the country, and the village of Shirakawa-go maintains a centuries-old method of dealing with winter. The farmhouses here are known for their *gassho zukuri* construction, steeply angled roofs designed to withstand the weight of snow that accumulated during the months when the roads out of the village were completely cut off and extended farm families took shelter. The huge roofs vary from two to three stories and use only thatch bound to thick oak frames to keep out rain and snow. The largest cluster of these traditional farmhouses, some of which are three centuries old, is in the Ogi-machi hamlet, which has 59. The area, which straddles Gifu and Toyama prefectures, is a World Heritage Site.

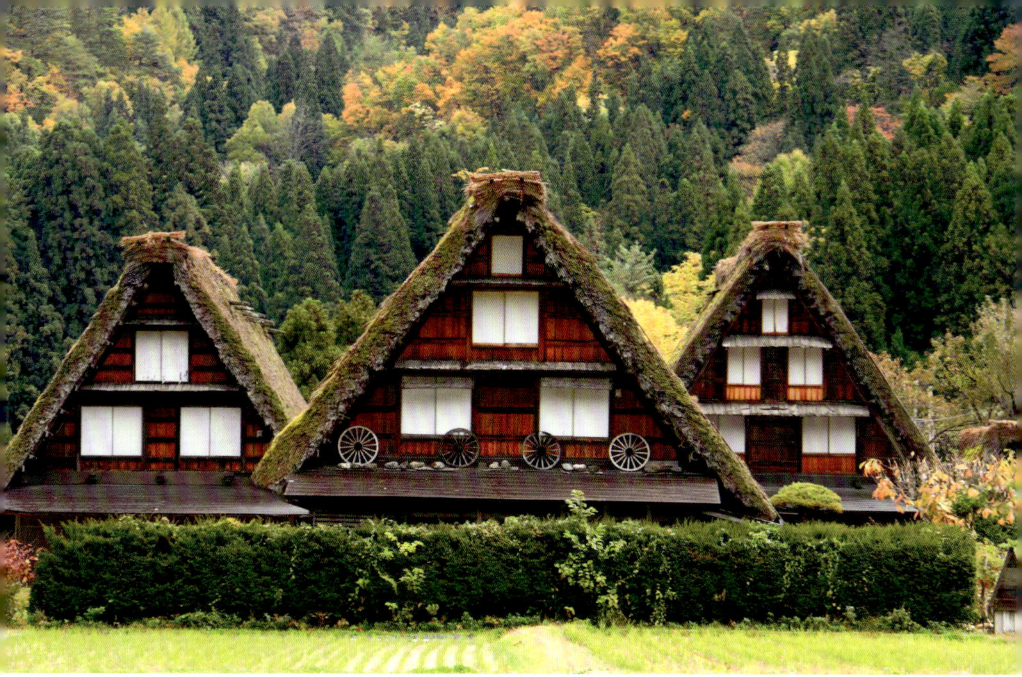

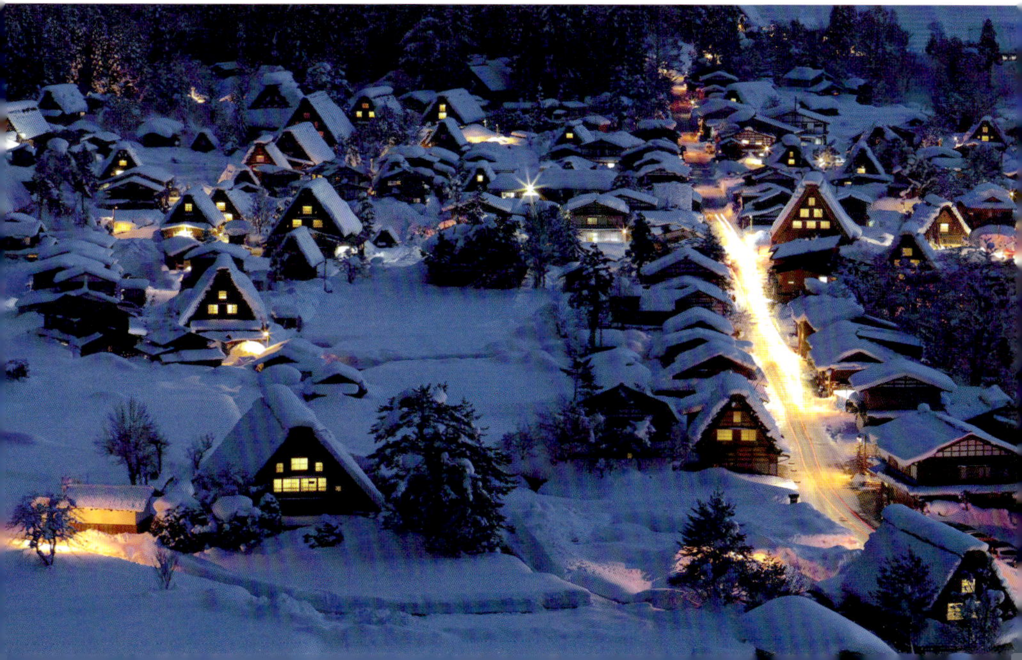

Takayama | GIFU

Many small towns are referred to as "little Kyotos," but this tranquil town in the heart of the isolated Hida Mountain Range has a rare charm that fully justifies a visit. The Sanmachi area is known for its rows of elegant traditional wood-lattice buildings, built and maintained by generations of prosperous merchants. The town is known for its popular Sanno Festival in April and Hachiman Festival in October, which feature parades of gorgeous floats, admired for their refined decorations and performances by sophisticated mechanical puppets.

Ukai | GIFU

Fishermen in Gifu developed a unique method for catching river fish called *ukai*, literally "cormorant fishing." They use the light of torches to attract fish toward their fishing boats. The fishermen then release several birds onto the surface of the water to dive for the fish. Once the birds catch the fish, they are unable to swallow it due to a loop around its neck. The fisherman reels in the successful cormorant, forces it to disgorge the fish, then drops it back into the water for another attempt. Nowadays, this traditional method is aimed at visitors from late spring through early autumn.

Mt. Fuji | SHIZUOKA

Mountain worshippers began climbing 3,776-meter-high Mt. Fuji in the Heian period as a religious rite. The mountain itself was considered a *kami* or deity. During the Edo period, groups called *Fuji-ko* collected money to pay for members to make the climb. During the official climbing season in July and August, climbers begin the five to six-hour climb in the middle of the night to watch the sunrise from the summit. Mt. Fuji is a UNESCO World Heritage Site.

Chabatake | SHIZUOKA

Buddhist monks brought the custom of drinking tea to Japan from China. Some 800 years ago, the Japanese acquired seeds and the knowledge necessary for cultivating the plants. The Makinohara hills in Shizuoka Prefecture are among the better-known tea-producing areas of the country. Tea plants seem to do well in hilly areas, which are unsuitable for rice production. The first-picked tea leaves of each season are known to be particularly delicious, but in some regions, the leaves may be harvested several times during the growing season.

Nagoya Castle | AICHI

The size of Nagoya Castle would have been sufficient to impress the feudal lords with the power of Tokugawa Ieyasu, who ordered them to contribute to its construction, but to add a touch of panache, it was topped with two golden statues of dolphin-like creatures. The original castle escaped dismantling when the Meiji government attempted to remove reminders of the former Tokugawa shogunate, but it was destroyed in the air raids of World War II. The donjon was reconstructed in 1959, complete with the golden statues on the top roof, which are now symbols of the city of Nagoya.

Kinki Area

Once known as Yamato, the Kinki region combines the ancient cultural and political center of Japan with the modern-day commercial and industrial center of western Japan. Until 1868, the Kyoto and Nara area was where the emperors resided, where Buddhism flourished and where traditional Japanese culture developed to its highest peak. Although it is no longer the political center of the country, it remains the cultural heart of traditional Japan. To the west, the port at Kobe and the factories at Osaka have the air of cities where production and trade are important daily tasks. They each have their own sense of style, cuisine preferences and lifestyle, unapologetic for being different from Tokyo and other eastern metropolises. Kinki has a deep religious history as the base for both the Ise Grand Shrines and the Buddhist strongholds at Mt. Koya and Mt. Hiei. Stretching from the Sea of Japan to the Kii Peninsula, the terrain is mountainous with small basins in between which make for high humidity during the summer months and occasional harsh cold in winter. The coastal plains along the Seto Inland Sea are comparatively mild, but the northern part of the region has extremely heavy snowfalls.

Kiyomizu-dera Temple | KYOTO

The magnificent hillside temple overlooks the Otowa Spring, whose "pure water", *kiyomizu*, was revealed to the priest Enchin Shonin in a dream. The main hall is shingled, unlike the usual tiled temple roofs, and in front of it extends its trademark platform, from which one can see both the spring and, to the west, the city of Kyoto.

Supported by 139 pillars, the platform of Kiyomizu-dera was constructed as a dance stage, which stands 13 meters above the hillside below. In the Edo period, the spring drew pilgrims who believed in its curative powers. Today the temple and the spring draw people from nations around the world who drink the water in hopes of health, success and longevity.

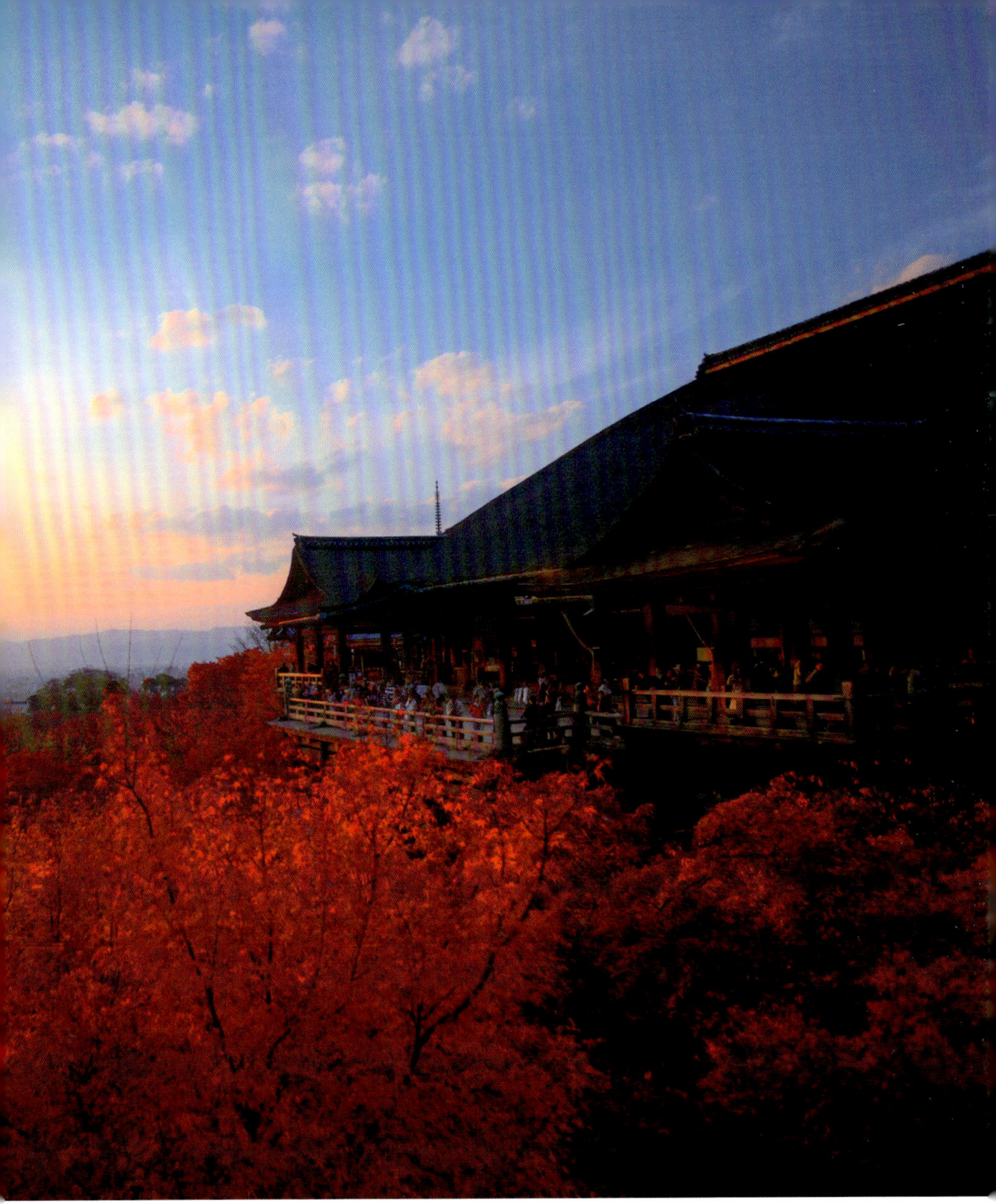

Fushimi Inari | KYOTO

Of the 40,000 some Shinto shrines around the country dedicated to the deity Inari, the Fushimi Inari Taisha, south of Kyoto, is far and away the most significant and the most impressive. Inari is the god of rice agriculture, prosperity and business, and its messenger is the fox, accounting for the white foxes that appear at the gate to most of the shrines. This shrine, however, is noted for its bronze foxes. It is especially well known for its tunnel of some 10,000 *torii* gates, each offered by a different donor.

Ryoan-ji Temple | KYOTO

Inspired by the profound teachings of Zen, the famous *karesansui* rock garden at Ryoan-ji is composed of fifteen stones of different sizes in carefully raked white gravel. The abstract arrangement permits—even demands—a variety of interpretations. What is not in doubt is that this confined space, the walls enclosing it and the trees beyond the yellowish-clay wall provide a superb setting for contemplation. The temple's coin-shaped water fountain bears a proscription that one ought to pursue learning not for profit but for its own sake. This is good advice for those who sit on the verandah contemplating the abstract garden.

Kinkaku-ji Temple | KYOTO

Once the villa of a court noble, Kinkaku-ji Temple became the political base of the third Ashikaga shogun, Yoshimitsu. After his death, it became a Zen temple, whose official name is Rokuon-ji. The Golden Pavilion, built in 1397, was destroyed by a deranged monk in 1950, reconstructed in 1955, and repaired in 1987 adding 200,000 sheets of gold leaf to the glowing structure. Each floor has a different design.

Ginkaku-ji Temple | KYOTO

The shogun Ashikaga Yoshimasa constructed the Ginkaku-ji, the Silver Pavilion, in the late 15th century. The original plan to cover it with silver leaf was never achieved. Nonetheless, the building is a superb example of refined taste and restrained expression. Among Yoshimasa's leisure pursuits was moon viewing. The light of the moon reflects off the pond and the carefully raked Sea of Silvery Sand appears to ripple in the silvery light of the moon.

Gion | KYOTO

Gion in Kyoto's Higashiyama district is known for the rows of traditional wooden houses with latticework doors and windows that line the streets leading to Yasaka-jinja Shrine. Shops in the area sell traditional Kyoto crafts, pottery, incense and the accessories that go with formal kimono. Once one of Kyoto's most prestigious night entertainment quarters, it retains a traditional elegance. In the evening, one may still spot geisha and apprentice *maiko* going to and from the centuries-old teahouses, *chaya*, to perform for guests.

Gion Matsuri, Yasaka Shrine | KYOTO

The Gion-matsuri Festival held in summer is famous for its procession of magnificent floats on which musicians play festival music with Japanese flutes, bells and drums.

Kinki Area 114

Arashiyama | KYOTO

Arashiyama in the western section of Kyoto is known for its cherry blossoms, autumn leaves, and the views of the Hozu-gawa River and Togetsu-kyo Bridge. The sites were lauded in classical poetry and they retain enormous visual appeal as well as being representative of Kyoto's aesthetic and spiritual character.

Togetsu Bridge | KYOTO

In the northwestern part of Kyoto, Arashiyama's scenery and atmosphere are superb in any season. Its focal point is the 155-meter Togetsu-kyo, the "Moon-Crossing Bridge," across the Katsura River, rebuilt in 1934 with reinforced concrete and cypress parapets. The bridge provides a panoramic view of Arashiyama, the small mountain south of the bridge, with cherry blossoms in spring and red and yellow leaves in autumn. To get a closer look at the natural beauty of the river, a trolley train runs along the beautiful gorge north of the bridge from Arashiyama Station.

Gozan no Okuribi | KYOTO

Throughout Japan during the period of Obon, families welcome the spirits of their ancestors with lanterns in the evening. Kyoto sends the spirits off in style by setting fire to bonfires in the shapes of Chinese characters such as *dai*, meaning "great," on Mt. Daimonji and four other mountains (the Gozan). These bonfires can be seen from all over the city on the evening of August 16, lighting the way (*okuribi*) for the spirits to return to their resting places.

Otagi Nenbutsu-ji Temple | KYOTO

Off the beaten path in the Arashiyama section of Kyoto is a pleasant countryside walk that leads from one temple famous for its elegant grove of bamboo to several others filled with stone Buddhist statuettes memorializing the deceased or stone statues called *rakan* that represent the disciples of Buddha. There are usually a symbolic 500 of the *rakan*, each with a different face and most appearing to laugh. Each August, candles are lit to illuminate the stone images creating a scene suggestive of the Buddhist Pure Land.

Ama-no-hashidate | KYOTO

Of the often-cited top three scenic spots in Japan, Ama-no-hashidate, "the bridge to heaven," is unique in being a sandbar covered with pine trees. The 3.6-kilometer-long natural phenomenon has been a motif in poetry and painting since ancient times. There are debates regarding the best point from which to look out over the sandbar, but the view from Mt. Monju-yama is said to look like a dragon flying up into the heavens. On summer nights, the "bridge" is lit with 170 torches, reflecting on the surface of the sea like fireworks.

Great Buddha, Todai-ji | NARA

Todai-ji Temple houses the world's largest bronze statue of Buddha inside the largest pre-modern wooden building. The 15-meter-high Vairocana Buddha was once plated with gold and it weighs over 500 tons. It has 110,000 tiles on the roof alone, each weighing 15 kilograms. Since its

Todai-ji Temple | NARA

Nara was the imperial capital from 710 to 784 and during those years, Buddhism became the religion of the court and the nation. In the center of Nara, is Todai-ji Temple, the head temple of the Kegon Sect. Founded by Emperor Shomu, the temple was intended to serve as the center of a network of temples around the nation to promote the well being of the nation. According to tradition, its construction costs nearly bankrupt the government. Nearby Nigatsu-do, "Second-Month Hall", is famous for its annual Omizu-tori, "drawing of sacred water", ceremony held at night.

Deer at Nara Park | NARA

The grassy wooded center of several World Heritage Sites, Nara Park extends about four kilometers from east to west, and about two kilometers from south to north. Within the general park area are the major destinations of Kofuku-ji Temple, Todai-ji Temple, Nigatsu-do Hall, Shoso-in Treasure Repository and Kasuga Taisha Shrine as well as small streams and ponds. In addition to human visitors who pass through, the permanent residents are some 1,500 basically tame deer, regarded as emissaries of the deity of the Kasuga Shrine. Stalls in the area sell deer crackers, *shika senbei*, for the tourists to donate to these residents.

completion in 752, the statue has been repeatedly repaired but the lotus petal base and the legs have survived from the original. The original building that housed it was a third larger, but even the current building from the mid-Edo period is impressive.

Kofuku-ji Temple | NARA

Once one of the great temples of Nara, Kofuku-ji Temple had more than 150 buildings within its precincts. It was the family temple of the Fujiwara, who virtually controlled the country for several centuries. There were once three main halls, but only the Tokondo, the East Main Hall, remains. The temple's five-story pagoda was first erected in 725 but the current one dates from 1426. The oldest building in the complex is the Northern Octagonal Hall from 1210.

Heijo-kyo Palace Site | NARA

In the early years of the country, the capital was moved each time a new emperor took the throne. At the start of the Nara period in 710, the capital was established at Heijo-kyo. The capital was moved to Kyoto in 794 and the original buildings of the Nara palace were lost. The magnificent temples on the outskirts of the former capital, however, survived and are part of Nara's much-visited sights. Recently parts of this previous palace have been reconstructed and are open to the public.

Mt. Yoshino-yama | NARA

According to legend, a seventh-century Buddhist priest named En-no-Ozunu planted cherry trees on Mt. Yoshino-yama in enormous numbers. There are some 30,000 trees in four distinct sections in rows up the mountain. As a result, the trees at the bottom of the mountain go into full blossom first, followed by the next section higher, until finally the top blooms. The pilgrimage routes from Mt. Yoshino-yama and Mt. Koya-san to Kumano are a cultural UNESCO World Heritage Site.

Shirahige-jinja Shrine | SHIGA

The head shrine of those dedicated to the deity Sarutahiko Okami is the Shirahige-jinja Shrine on Lake Biwa in Shiga Prefecture. Its autumn festival features a ceremony called Naruko-mairi in which children at the age of two are brought to the shrine and given a name by the shrine's god. It is said that calling the child by this name for several days will ensure the protection of the god for the child's safety and a happy life. The *torii* gate of the shrine stands just offshore in the lake itself.

Chikubu-shima Island, Lake Biwa | SHIGA

In pre-modern times, Lake Biwa was the site of many important historical and cultural events and in the northern part of the lake, the small Chikubu-shima Island is still known for Hogon-ji Temple and its statue of Kannon, famous as the 30th temple of the area's Kannon Temple Pilgrimage. With the exception of the winter months, boats reach the island from several ports along the shore of the lake.

Dotonbori | OSAKA

The main entertainment district of Osaka and one of the most recognizable arrays of neon, lights and images in the country, Dotonbori is packed with pachinko parlors, inexpensive izakaya, bars, theaters and significantly risqué entertainments. The Dotonbori Canal and the main road leading from Nanba Station are the central area for restaurants. Drift off into the side streets and the population of touts holding menues increases. Regardless of budget, there is something for everyone in the stimulating part of Osaka, whose inhabitants are thought to be especially interested in food and a good time.

Meotoiwa | MIE

The small resort town of Futamigaura, on Ise Bay, is noted for its *Meotoiwa*, two "wedded rocks" bound by sacred ropes called *shimenawa*. The rocks were once thought to resemble the deities Izanagi and Izanami, who, according to the *Kojiki*, were the main creators of the land of Japan. The nearby Okitama Shrine adds further symbolism to the meaning of the rocks with its assembly of fertility symbols.

Kinki Area 126

Ise Jingu | MIE

Ise Shrine in Mie Prefecture, is one of the most important Shinto shrines in the country. The Outer Shrine, *Geku*, was established in the fifth century. It enshrines Toyouke no Omikami, the god of food, clothing and housing. Each of the main shrine buildings is rebuilt every twenty years on an adjacent lot. The old shrine is taken down and the space is left open. This regular rebuilding is part of a belief in the renewal of nature.

Ise Jingu Naiku | MIE

The Inner Shrine, *Naiku*, established in the third century enshrines Amaterasu, the Sun Goddess, who is represented by a sacred mirror. The mirror is considered one of the three sacred regalia, *sanshu no jingi*.

Ago-wan Bay | MIE

Ago-wan Bay in the southern part of the Shima Peninsula has an intricate coastline and more than 50 islands of various sizes. Only two of the islands, Kashiko-jima and Mazaki-jima are inhabited. The bay is famous as the first area in the country to successfully cultivate pearls. The surface of the sea between the smaller islands is dotted with the floating oyster racks that yield the pearls that make the bay one of the largest cultured pearl producers in Japan. In addition, the bay produces laver (*nori*), clams, and Iwa-gaki oysters.

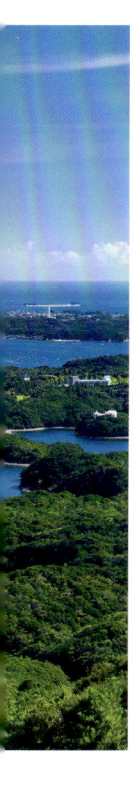

Old Kumano Roads | MIE

Some of the oldest surviving religious practices are based in the Kumano area in the Kii peninsula, which includes Wakayama and Mie prefectures. The network of ancient pilgrimage routes running along the coast and leading through the forested mountains connecting the three Kumano Grand Shrines is known collectively as the Kumano Old Roads, *Kumano Kodo*. During the medieval period, these roads were supported by guides and places to stay overnight, as the pilgrimage from Kyoto took some 40 days.

Kumano Hayatama Taisha Reisai | WAKAYAMA

The Hongu, Hayatama and Nachi shrines are the three central destinations. The Hongu Grand Shrine is the focus of the whole area. Kumano Nachi Grand Shrine originated in worship of the Nachi Waterfall, which falls some 133 meters from a forested cliff. The Hayatama Grand Shrine is the site of a night fire festival in February when men carrying torches lit from a sacred fire burst out of the shrine gate and carry them down the slope.

Old Kumano Roads | WAKAYAMA

The Kumano area's religious bases are multiple. Buddhism is mixed with Shinto elements, with local Shinto deities regarded as manifestations of universal Buddhist deities. Those are further mixed with the practices of mountain ascetics known as *yamabushi* and prehistoric nature worship. There is no clear line between the sources, but the overall atmosphere is intensely spiritual, in addition to being a place to enjoy nature.

Hashiguiiwa | WAKAYAMA

On the southern coast of Wakayama Prefecture, near Cape Shiono-misaki, the warm current that flows along the archipelago passes closest to Honshu, making the area a rich fishing ground. The coastline near the cape has high cliffs, peculiarly shaped rocks that are typical of a saw-toothed coastline. Hashiguiiwa, natural stone pillars that seem like pilings of some long disappeared bridge, is a destination for photographers who find the rocks a fascinating subject.

Mt. Koya | WAKAYAMA

Founder of the Shingon sect of Buddhism in Japan, Kukai was granted the leadership of the To-ji Temple in Kyoto, one of the two most powerful Buddhist institutions in Heian-kyo, the capital city, which is present-day Kyoto. In addition, he established this temple complex on the plateau of Mt. Koya (Koya-san) as a training center for esoteric practices, far removed from the distractions of the capital.

Known posthumously as Kobo Daishi, Kukai's mausoleum is in the sacred Oku-no-in Cemetery across the Gobyo-bashi Bridge. The path through the cemetery is lined with statues of Jizo, the bodhisattva who is held to be the guardian of children, a protector of travelers, and a guide to the spirits of the dead. Major services are held in the main hall of Kongobu-ji, but the whole area exudes spirituality. This World Heritage Site is a superb location for an overnight stay and an opportunity to enjoy the vegetarian *shojin-ryori* that the monks in training eat daily.

Himeji-jo Castle | HYOGO

The complex layout of the exterior and interior walls, gates, firing ports and deadend approaches made the Himeji-jo Castle almost invincible when it was completed in 1609. Unlike many other castles, it survived the Meiji period destruction of castles and aerial bombing of World War II, leaving it as arguably the finest remaining castle in the country. After a five-year renovation, the elegant castle, now has new roof tiles and repainted white plastered earthen walls and donjon. Also known as the White Egret Castle, the castle is a national treasure in addition to being a World Heritage site.

Takeda-jo Castle | HYOGO

Known as the "Castle in the Sky" and "Japan's Machu Picchu" due to the clouds that often form below the site during autumn and winter, the remains of Takeda-jo Castle in Asago City, Hyogo Prefecture, are included in the list of the 100 outstanding castles of Japan. While the castle was abandoned more than 400 years ago, impressive stonewalls stretch 400 meters from north to south and 100 meters from east to west suggest its size.

Ijinkan, Kobe | HYOGO

Kobe is known around the world for its tender, marbled beef, which ranks at the top of all true *wagyu*, Japanese beef. Although one might not wish to pay the high prices for authentic Kobe beef, one can enjoy the sights of the Kitano district of Kobe on the slopes of Mt. Rokko-san. The early foreign traders who the government allowed to operate in the Kobe area after the Meiji Restoration chose Kitano to build their enclave of homes and churches. Several "foreign residences" (*ijinkan*) remain today and they attract visitors who also drop in the boutiques and cafes that have opened in this upscale neighborhood.

Chugoku Area

Literally "the middle country", the Chugoku region consists of the whole western end of Honshu, with Kurashiki, Okayama and Hiroshima being its three prominent cities. The region is divided into two sub-regions, the northern half being San'in, "shadow of the mountains," a rural area facing the Sea of Japan with a harsh climate and less accessibility. The southern half of Chugoku facing the Inland Sea is called San'yo, "the sunny side of the mountains," and it is a comparatively industrialized area. The majority of the population in Chugoku resides in San'yo, mostly in the cities mentioned above and in other port towns along the coast. Thanks to its warm, dry climate, this area is an important producer of rice, citrus fruits and grapes. Among the region's highlights are the Izumo Grand Shrine on the north coast and the Itsukushima Shrine in the Inland Sea near Hiroshima.

Chugoku Area 138

Itsukushima Shrine | HIROSHIMA

A sacred site since 593, Miya-jima Island is known for the Itsukushima Shrine with its famous *torii* gateway. The shrine complex of 56 wooden structures is built out into an inlet so that at high tide, it appears to float on the surface of the water. Precisely why it was positioned that way is unclear, but it is the only such shrine in the country. Even the floorboards of the buildings were constructed with gaps to relieve pressure from the waters at high tide. The complex includes three types of stages—one for ceremonies, another for stately *kagura* court dances, and a third for Noh performances.

The Grand Torii is the shrine's most distinguishing feature not just because of its 16-meter height but because of its location in the sea off Miyajima Island. The current scarlet gate was originally erected there to welcome worshippers who would have arrived by boat, because according to one tradition it was not permitted for them to defile the sacred island by stepping directly onto the shore. The current *torii* dates from 1875 and it is made from ancient camphor wood, which resists decay. At low tide, one can walk out to the gate; at high tide, it would be possible to sail through the gate.

Onomichi | HIROSHIMA

This ancient port on the Seto Inland Sea near Hiroshima City has long been a center of commerce and shipbuilding. The steep face of the wooded Mt. Senko-ji above the port is covered with some 25 temples for those who enjoy a leisurely walk. A hill-top observatory, accessible by ropeway, provides an impressive view of the town and the narrow Onomichi Channel that separates it from the nearest island. Onomichi is also the base of a system of bridges that cross the Inland Sea to Shikoku.

Tomonoura | HIROSHIMA

A prosperous port since ancient times, Tomonoura's unique circular harbor makes the town and the port a picturesque old-fashioned fishing townscape. Facing the Seto Inland Sea, the town and its rustic old houses have been used as a film location for Japanese and foreign films. It is also known for its *homeishu*, the local medicinal liquor.

Genbaku Dome | HIROSHIMA

When an atomic bomb was detonated above Hiroshima on August 6, 1945, it instantly killed 100,000 people. It exploded over the former Hiroshima Prefectural Industrial Promotion Hall, which was surmounted by a metal-framed dome. That building, now the Genbaku Dome, is a monument to remind humankind of the terrible destruction that nuclear weapons can cause. It is the only structural ruin left erect in the city. Across the river are the Peace Memorial Museum and the Flame of Peace.

Tottori Sand Dunes | TOTTORI

Located in Japan's least populated prefecture, the *Tottori-sakyu*, the Tottori Sand Dunes, are a product of strong winds, sand brought down the Sendai-gawa River, and a vigorous churning of the waters offshore. This 10-kilometer stretch of coastline is part of the windswept coastline of San-in Kaigan National Park. At times the dunes rise some 50 meters above the sea and in places are almost 2 kilometers wide. The dunes were used as a location for Teshigahara Hiroshi's 1964 classic film, based on Abe Kobo's novel, *The Woman in the Dunes*.

Sakaiminato | TOTTORI

In the port city of Sakaiminato some 100 bronze statues of *yokai*, the sort of spirit monsters created by Shigeru Mizuki, a Japanese manga author best known for *GeGeGe-no-Kitaro*, line the street named after the author. The city was known as a fishing port and trade port with the continent. Reminders of its long history can be found in the traditional white-walled storehouses and *nagayamon*, a gate of tenements. The Yodoe-cho district is known for its clear water, which bubbles up at several locations.

Matsuba Crab | TOTTORI

Gourmets may debate which of the Sea of Japan products is best, but the snow crab known locally as Matsuba crab is one of the leading contenders. Caught from November through March, the tender meat is boiled, grilled and served as sashimi. Matsuba *kani miso*, crab innards, is considered a special treat.

Mt. Daisen | TOTTORI

Mt. Daisen, in western Tottori, is actually the name of a chain of eight mountains with Mt. Tsuru-ga-mine, 1,711 meters above sea level, as its highest peak. There are several observation spots, including one at the Kagikake Pass, where you can enjoy a panoramic view of virgin beech and oak tree forests. In the vicinity are facilities such as a blueberry farm for tourists, a dude ranch for enjoying a barbeque, a athletic field facility, and a horseback riding center for long-distance rides through the woods.

Izumo Taisha Shrine | SHIMANE

Izumo Shrine (*Izumo Taisha* or *Oyashiro*) in Shimane Prefecture, enshrines the deity which protects agriculture, marriage and good fortune. The current shrine is 24 meters high but archaeologists believe that the ancient shrine reached almost 96 meters in height. In ancient times, people believed that all of the *kami* around the country gathered at Izumo in October, to confer about their local regions. Today the shrine is popular for *enmusubi*, making or strengthening marital bonds, symbolized by the *shimenawa*, a huge braided straw rope that hangs in front of the shrine.

Iwami Silver Mine | SHIMANE

The Iwami Silver Mine, in Shimane Prefecture, was in active production between 1526 and 1923. In the late 16th century, Japanese silver made up approximately one-third of the world's production. Half of that silver was produced at this mine. Silver being important in international trade, the Tokugawa shogunate was quick to gain direct control of the mine and the routes along which the extracted silver was carried to small ports on the Sea of Japan, Hakata and the world beyond. To protect the workers against harsh, dangerous working conditions, protective shrines were built in the area and there is a temple with 500 arhats.

Lake Shinji-ko | SHIMANE

Lake Shinji-ko, west of the pleasant small city of Matsue, is known for the fish and shellfish which flourish in the confluence of seawater and freshwater in the lake. The waters yield icefish, eels, perch, prawns and carp. Fishermen in small boats also use a pole with a claw-shaped basket on the end to harvest Yamato clams. The island of Yomegashima seen from the eastern shore of the lake is beautiful at sunset.

Tsuwano | SHIMANE

Off the beaten track is the town of Tsuwano, birthplace of Mori Ogai, one of the two great writers of the Meiji period. He spent the first years of his life here and one of his tombs is here. Despite his acclaim as surgeon-general of the Imperial Army and his fame as a writer, translator and critic, he wanted only his birth name engraved on this tombstone: Mori Rintaro. Thanks to the stucco-and-tile walls that once enclosed samurai estates and the brocade carp and iris-filled canals flowing along the streets make a stroll through the mountain town is a memorable experience.

Akiyoshidai Plateau | YAMAGUCHI

Under the rolling grass-covered upland peppered by limestone outcroppings of Akiyoshidai Plateau is an enormous lime grotto. The Akiyoshi-do limestone cave is one of the largest in the world, extending more than ten kilometers deep, contains stalactites, stalagmites, rivers, deep pools and waterfalls. The main passage is 90 meters at its widest and 30 meters at its highest point.

Kintai-kyo Bridge | YAMAGUCHI

An hour away from Hiroshima, the small city of Iwakuni is known for its cormorant fishing and the views from the hilltop, where a reconstruction of Iwakuni Castle is located. The main draw, however, is the Kintai-kyo Bridge, whose first iteration was constructed by the feudal lord Kikkawa Hiroyoshi in 1673. The graceful five-arched bridge has been restored several times over the centuries, but its high arches still make an impressive sight over the wide river.

Tsunoshima | YAMAGUCHI

The small island of Tsunoshima in northwest Yamaguchi Prefecture is surrounded by the Japan Sea. It was once a considerably remote location, but in 2000, a 1,780-meter-long bridge connected it to the mainland. That bridge stands as the longest of the public road bridges in the county, second only to one in Okinawa. The island has gained some fame recently as a location for television dramas and movies.

Kurashiki | OKAYAMA

The preserved area of Kurashiki, called Bikan, has canals, bridges and white-stucco old warehouses with crisscrossed raised diagonals of white mortar covered with brown and black tiles. The warehouses once housed the cotton, textiles, rice and sugar that passed along the Inland Sea to and from Osaka. An ivy-covered facility that was once a weaving mill now houses several museums, a central courtyard and a beer garden. Several granaries retaining their original white-walled Edo-period appearance have been converted into the Kurashiki Folk Craft Museum.

Shikoku Area

The smallest of the four main islands of Japan, due to its high mountains and steep slopes, Shikoku has limited agriculture, a comparatively small population and restricted public transportation. It subtropical climate makes for short winters and long, hot summers, due in part to the Kuroshio current of the Pacific which flows along its southern coast. The southern side of the island gets considerable rainfall in the summer and faces frequent typhoons. The island is known for the famous pilgrimage route of 88 temples and shrines related to Kukai, also known as Kobo Daishi, the ninth-century founder of Esoteric Buddhism in Japan.

Shikoku 88 Pilgrimage

The Shikoku Pilgrimage is a route that links 88 specific places of worship believed to have some connection with Kukai, also known as Kobo Daishi. Kukai was born in Zentsu-ji, in Shikoku, and after studying in China, he established the esoteric Shingon Sect of Buddhism on Mt. Koya. It is not surprising that a cult and pilgrimage circuit developed on the island where he was born. The pilgrimage is 1,400 kilometers long and includes eighty Shingon temples and eight temples of other sects.

The traditional way is to walk the entire route clockwise, offering prayers at each of the temples. In spring, when the weather is mostly cooperative, this takes about six weeks. Some modern-day pilgrims make the circuit in sections spread over several years and others travel the route by bus in ten to twelve days.

Sanuki Udon | KAGAWA

The Sanuki region of Kagawa Prefecture is famous as the place of origin of wheat-flour noodles called Sanuki udon, known for its strong body and smooth texture. A light kelp-based soup seasoned with mild soy sauce is poured over the noodles, which can be garnished with leeks, ginger or sesame as well. Other toppings include vegetable and seafood tempura. This "Udon Kingdom" in Kagawa has a wide variety of shops from fancy to self-service, and shops around the country try to mimic this delicious variety of udon.

Uzushio | TOKUSHIMA

Rapid tidal currents and the changes in water levels that result are responsible for one of the well-visited sights in Shikoku. In the Naruto Strait between northeastern Shikoku and Awaji Island, just before and after the ebb and flow of the tides, the swift currents form whirlpools of various sizes. The Naruto Ohashi Bridge has an observatory with panes of glass in the floor, from which you can look straight down to the whirlpools some 50 meters below.

Kazura-bashi | TOKUSHIMA

Tokushima, at the eastern end of Shikoku, is known for its castle ruins, its Bunraku puppet (*ningyo joruri*) tradition and the Awa Odori festival, held in mid-August, when dancers take to the streets in traditional costume to frenetically expel the dullness of summer heat. Away from the city, however, one finds deep forests and reminders of rural life like the *Kazura-bashi*, a 50-meter-long bridge made of vines and bamboo that spans the Iyadani-kei Gorge. Rustic though it may seem, it is rebuilt every three years and is reinforced with steel cables.

Oboke | TOKUSHIMA

Between Tokushima and Kochi, the road and rail lines pass through an area around Oboke Koboke where swift-flowing rivers cut deep valleys in the red earth and the foliage is lush and verdant. The green vines that climb the trees have been used to construct the bridge that crosses a particularly deep gorge along the way.

Awa-Odori | TOKUSHIMA

Tokushima is known for its mid-summer extravaganza: the Awa Odori Festival, which dates back over 400 years. The exciting dancing of this festival is so popular that it is performed around Japan and even abroad at events like the Rio Carnival. The Awa Odori Festival takes place over four days in the middle of August each year to welcome the souls of the ancestors during Obon, and venues throughout the city are filled with dancers and over 1.3 million visitors. Awa Odori is characterized by irregular steps and an energetic up-tempo rhythm played by gongs, flutes, drums and three-stringed instruments.

Dogo Onsen | EHIME

The centerpiece of this hot spring town on the edge of Matsuyama City is the three-story, multi-roofed castle-style Honkan, which was constructed in 1894. It is said to have been frequented by the Meiji writer Natsume Soseki, who praised its healing powers, and more recently it was the model for the Miyazaki Hayao anime *Spirited Away*. The building maintains a late 19th-century aura in the changing rooms and the baths themselves, and patrons from the local community and from far away all enjoy the waters.

Ehime Mikan | EHIME

Ehime Prefecture has produced citrus for over a century, succeeding because of its mild climate and relatively fair weather throughout the year. The citrus fruits produced on steep slopes with well-drained soil are full of minerals and receive just the right amount of moisture from the winds blowing across the Seto Inland Sea. *Ehime mikan*, a kind of mandarin orange, are available almost all year. Other varieties include *ponkan*, *amanatsu* and *iyokan*.

Katsura-hama | KOCHI

To the south of the city of Kochi on Urado Bay is Katsura-hama Beach, known for its contrast of pine forests and rocky coast. Also situated on this part of the bay is the Sakamoto Ryoma Memorial Museum, which honors the visionary Ryoma who was born in Kochi and was involved in the attempts to overthrow the Tokugawa Shogunate before being assassinated at the age of 33. Ryoma remains popular for his character and his way of life.

Cape Ashizuri | KOCHI

The southernmost tip of Shikoku is comparatively untamed country. The road through the cape's middle reaches the lighthouse at the tip and Kongofuku-ji Temple, one stage of the Shikoku Pilgrimage of 88 sacred sites, whose origins date back more than a thousand years. The narrow promontory is rich in subtropical vegetation and is famed for its panoramic views of the Pacific Ocean.

Kyushu Area

The Kyushu region is the third largest and the southernmost of the four major islands of the country. In addition to the main island, it includes a large number of small islands where fish and shellfish are cultivated. The mountainous interior combines volcanoes like Mt. Aso, hot springs and coastal plains. It has a subtropical climate with heavy rainfall. It is particularly known for sweet potatoes, citrus fruit and stock farming. Being closest to China and Korea, Kyushu long served as the main gate for cultural influences from the continent, including the culture of rice cultivation. Nagasaki also served for centuries as the exclusive port for trade with the West.

Nakasu Yatai | FUKUOKA

An island in the middle of the Nakagawa River, Nakasu is the main entertainment district of Fukuoka. At the end of the day, local people and visitors head to Nakasu for the Fukuoka trademark establishments: pushcart stalls called *yatai* that are set up to provide inexpensive fare in a friendly, casual atmosphere. At the top of the menus are *motsu-nabe* (beef or pork intestines cooked with miso and vegetables in a hotpot) and the famous Hakata *tonkotsu* (boiled pork bone) ramen.

Moji-ko Port | FUKUOKA

Moji-ko Port flourished following its 1889 designation as a special national port for exporting coal and other products. Close to China, it served as a trading port making an important contribution to the modernization of Japan. Times have changed but architectural reminders like the former Moji Customs Building from 1912, the wooden Moji Station building from 1914, and the former Osaka Shosen Building from 1917 in the Moji-ko Port Retro Area remain as symbols and attractions. Across the Kanmon Strait is Shimonoseki, connected to Moji by the 3,461-meter-long Kanmon Tunnel, one fifth of which is below the strait.

Dazaifu Tenmangu Shrine | FUKUOKA

Dazaifu was for a long time the administrative center of Kyushu, a center of trade with Korea and China. It is also associated with the statesman Sugawara no Michizane who challenged the powerful Fujiwara family within the imperial court in Kyoto. He was falsely accused of plotting against the throne and was assigned to Daizaifu, in far away Kyushu, where he died in 903 A.D., bemoaning his unjust exile. The Dazaifu Tenmangu Shrine is dedicated to the slandered courtier.

Yoshinogari Site | SAGA

During the Yayoi Period (c. 300 BCE–300 CE), this moat-enclosed area was the site of a complex culture, which was discovered in 1986 and has been the subject of serious study since. Remains and relics from Yayoi culture have been excavated and replicas of the buildings have been constructed to show what archaeologists believe the original residences, gathering places, storehouses and defenses looked like.

Karatsu Kunchi | SAGA

The Karatsu Kunchi festival held at Karatsu-jinja Shrine has a history of some four centuries. The November festival features gigantic floats, weighing two to four tons and standing almost seven meters tall, which are lacquered and covered with gold and silver leaf. These masterpieces are images of samurai helmets, fish, and flying dragons. The oldest is a red lion float which was originally constructed in 1819. The highlight is on the second day when participants haul the 14 floats through the sand at Nishi-no-hama Beach to the accompaniment of shouts, flutes and drums.

Hamanoura | SAGA

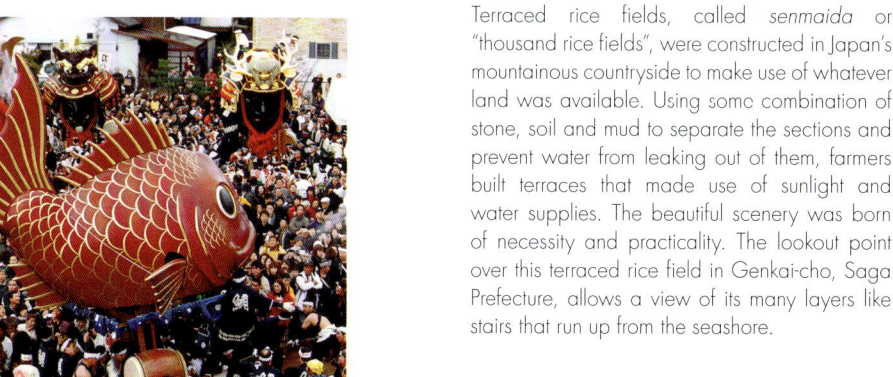

Terraced rice fields, called *senmaida* or "thousand rice fields", were constructed in Japan's mountainous countryside to make use of whatever land was available. Using some combination of stone, soil and mud to separate the sections and prevent water from leaking out of them, farmers built terraces that made use of sunlight and water supplies. The beautiful scenery was born of necessity and practicality. The lookout point over this terraced rice field in Genkai-cho, Saga Prefecture, allows a view of its many layers like stairs that run up from the seashore.

Mt. Aso | KUMAMOTO

In virtually the center of the island of Kyushu, Mt. Aso features one of the world's largest calderas, 18 kilometers by 25 kilometers. The basin-shaped valley is home to tens of thousands of people and has fertile farmland. The crater contains five volcanic cones, one of which, Nakadake, is still active. It spews yellow sulfurous gas, but remains stable enough that tourists are generally allowed to visit the edge and look down into the core. Apart from this activity, the main movement is by the horses and dairy cows who feed on the emerald-green slopes of the other cones.

Tenku no Michi | KUMAMOTO

Tenku no michi, the "road through the sky", along the edge of the crater of Mt. Aso is a short loop that seems to go straight out into the sea of clouds that settle in the crater during certain periods in early autumn. The road actually leads through pastureland along what is "Milk Road" on most maps, but the surreal curve in the road has come to be known as a road that leads to and even through the heavens. Some call it the Raputa Road, after the Studio Ghibli film "Castle in the Sky", about a legendary floating city.

Kyushu Area

Kumamoto Castle | KUMAMOTO

Completed in 1607 by Kato Kiyomasa, this castle subsequently became the seat of power of the Hosokawa clan. The original was destroyed during the Satsuma Rebellion of 1877, when rebels against the imperial forces who came to power in 1868 made a final stand here before they surrendered and the castle was destroyed. The imperial army's use of Western cannons did serious damage but the walls basically survived. The massive stone walls—concave to prevent anyone from scaling them—are 5.3 kilometers in circumference and protect the soaring black-lacquered central keep. Reconstruction of this impressive castle was completed in 1960.

Tsujun-kyo Bridge | KUMAMOTO

The largest stone aqueduct in Japan, the Tsujun-kyo Bridge in Yamato, Kumamoto Prefecture, was a major architectural accomplishment in its day. Completed in 1854, it is 84 meters long and its arch spans just over 27 meters. It was planned by the head of a local village with the help of several dozen stonemasons and local farmers to bring water into the high Shiroito Plateau for farming. It is still a functioning aqueduct and in the agricultural off-season water is sometimes discharged for the enjoyment of visitors.

Peace Park | NAGASAKI

The U.S. dropped a second atom bomb on August 9, 1945, on Nagasaki. A decade later, the Statue of Peace, cast by Seibo Mitamura, was erected in the Nagasaki Peace Park. Not far from the statue is the Nagasaki Atomic Bomb Museum, whose exhibits show the enormity of the impact of the explosion. In the nearby Hypocenter Park, a memorial marks the exact site above which the bomb was detonated.

Gunkan-jima Island | NAGASAKI

Although its official name is Ha-shima Island, it is commonly known as Gunkan-jima Island, after the Japanese name for battleship. The island was once the site of an underwater mining operation and a town with several thousand residents. Coal was mined at 1,000 meters under the sea here, yielding a significant annual output. The multiple high-rise housing units on the island employed some of the most advanced construction methods of the times. The mine itself ceased operations in 1974 and the entire island was abandoned.

Kyushu Area | 170

Glover House | NAGASAKI

In 1859 an enterprising Scotsman named Thomas Glover arrived in Nagasaki and immediately became involved in a variety of businesses. Glover operated a coalmine, founded the first modern shipyard in Japan, supplied weapons to the Satsuma clan in southern Kyushu and established Japan's Kirin beer brewery. The Glover House, built in 1863, evokes an era when Western architecture and lifestyle were of great interest to the Japanese. Several other merchant houses have been relocated to the Glover Garden, which surrounds the house itself, making the area a pocket of 19th-century Western culture overlooking Nagasaki Bay.

Kujukushima | NAGASAKI

Although the name implies that there are ninety-nine islands in this group off the coast of Nagasaki prefecture, there are some two hundred of them, and they have a complex history. They were among the first islands where European missionaries landed in the 16th century as well as a base for the *wako* pirates who raided coastal cities throughout the region. The calm seas between the islands are now a rich breeding ground for oysters and pearls.

Nagasaki Kakure Kirishitan | NAGASAKI

Catholic missionaries arrived in Japan in the middle of the 16th century hoping to convert the locales and they had a degree of success in western Japan, especially western Kyushu. When the Tokugawa shogunate expelled the foreign missionaries and repeatedly suppressed the baptized Japanese converts, some of the faithful went underground as "hidden Christians", continuing their faith among themselves, making statues of Maria that looked like the Buddhist Bodhisattva Kannon. With no priests and no printed texts, their entire body of doctrine and liturgy was passed down by word of mouth. Their existence was made known in the mid-19th century, when some believers came forward.

Sakurajima | KAGOSHIMA

Japan has 110 active volcanoes, seven percent of the world's total. Across the bay from the Kagoshima, the southernmost large city in Kyushu, Sakurajima is one of the most active, a volcano which spews ash and smoke over the local area on a regular basis. A violent eruption in 1914 buried over 1,000 homes in villages around the mountain, but during the last half-century the eruptions only cause minor inconveniences to Kagoshima residents. This deposits a layer of ash on cars, streets, and farm crops and occasionally makes holes with falling rocks.

Ferries make a regular trip across the bay to visit the volcano several times an hour, and when conditions are safe—which is generally the case—it is possible to go up to an observation platform on the side of the volcano.

Kyushu Area 174

Ibusuki | KAGOSHIMA

On the Satsuma Peninsula in Kagoshima Prefecture, the city is known for its group of hot springs. Underground hot springs warm the sand, and visitors cover themselves in the sand to improve circulation, increase perspiration and relax to the sound of the waves along the shore.

Yaku-shima | KAGOSHIMA

South of the city of Kagoshima and lying at the east end of the Okinawan archipelago, mountainous Yaku-shima Island is covered by a semitropical forest with trees as old as the country of Japan. At the center of the island, one of the wettest places in Japan, are several enormous *yaku-sugi* (Cryptomeria japonica, Yakushima cedars) which are at least 1,000 years old. The oldest cryptomeria tree, known as *Jomon-Sugi*, is estimated to be well over 2,000 years old.

Tanegashima | KAGOSHIMA

In 1543 shipwrecked Portuguese introduced muskets to this long narrow island south of Kagoshima City in southern Kyushu. These weapons, and their Japanese offspring known as *Tanegashima* or *teppo*, changed the nature of warfare among the feudal lords of Japan. Today the island is known as the home of Japan's Space Center, from which rockets carrying satellites are occasionally launched, and as a haven for laid-back surfers.

Takachiho-kyo Gorge | MIYAZAKI

This gorge carved by the Gokase-gawa River is known for its seven-kilometer stretch of sheer cliff walls formed of columnar joints, the Manaino-taki Falls and for its autumn foliage. The area itself is associated with the mythic beginnings of Japan as recorded in the ancient texts of the *Kojiki* (712) and the *Nihon Shoki* (720).

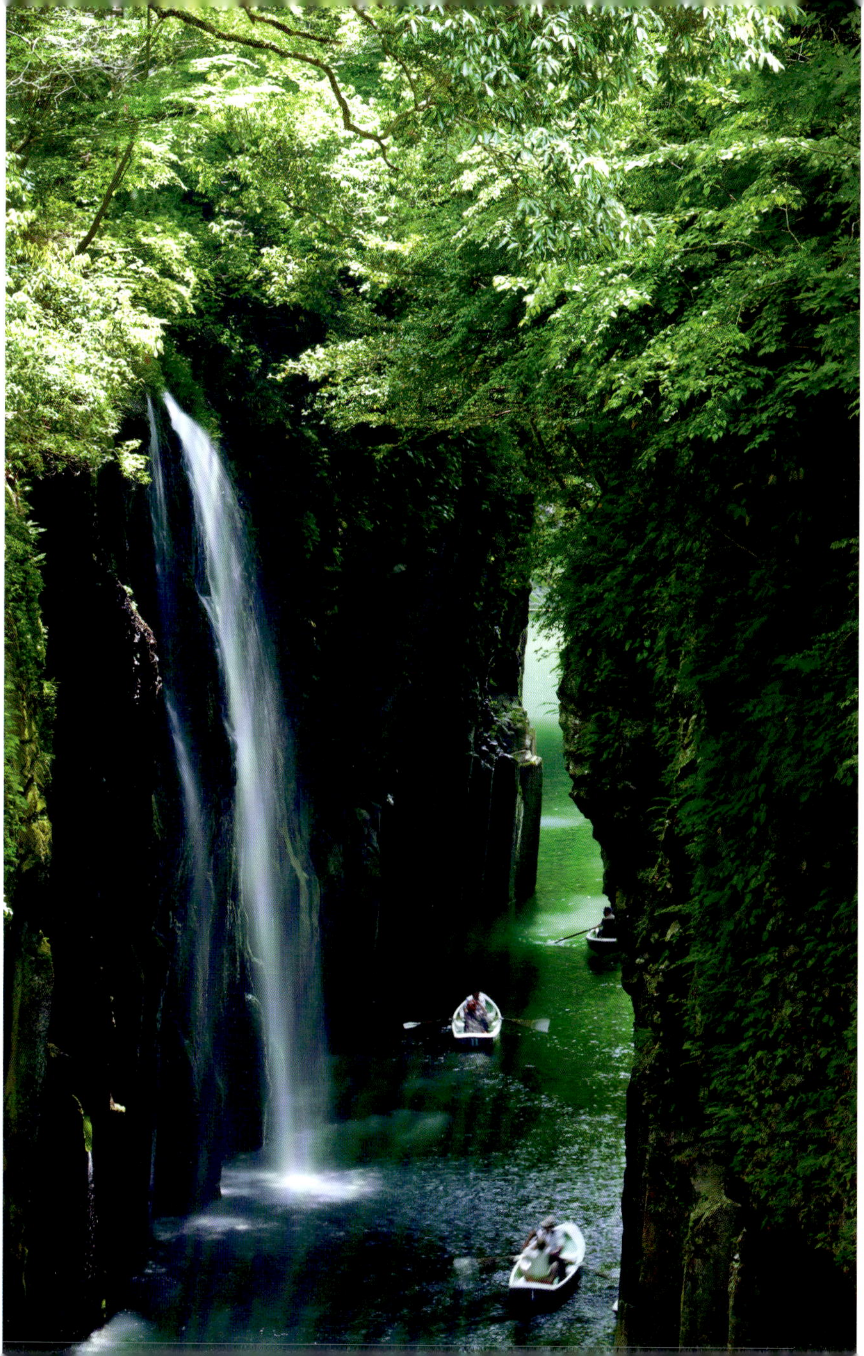

Beppu Hot Spring | OITA

The celebrated eight hot springs of Beppu put out the greatest volume of water in Japan. The city offers a century-old public bath and a chance to be covered to the neck with hot sand for ten minutes to improve circulation and to rejuvenate. Nearby in Kannawa is the Jigoku Meguri, which is a circuit of nine "hells" that are for viewing rather than suffering. They include bubbling mud springs, gurgling springs with reddish water nicknamed "pond of blood", a percolating blue-green spring, and even a geyser.

Okinawa Area

The Okinawan archipelago was an independent country known as the Ryukyu Kingdom from 1429 to 1879. Due to its strategic location along trading routes between Japan, China and Southeast Asia, it developed a unique culture borrowing from all of its neighbors. When the Ryukyu Kingdom was unified in 1429, the royal family built a castle on a small hill overlooking the present city of Naha to show its power over the islands. Shuri Castle became the residence of the kings and served as the site for religious rituals. It became the political and administrative center of the kingdom. Okinawa is subtropical and consists of some 60 islands, known collectively as the Ryukyu Islands. Agriculture is limited to sugarcane, pineapple and vegetables and the main industry is tourism. The Okinawan people have preserved their ancestors' religious festivals, music, traditional foods and historic sites.

Okinawa Area 180

Shisa

Traditional Okinawan architecture attempted to keep the house roofs from blowing away in the frequent typhoons with white plaster covering the red tiles. As a talisman against evil spirits, the Okinawans added a *shisa*, a guardian lion.

Shuri Castle

In 1945, all that remained of the castle were portions of the wall and a damaged gate. The ornate Chinese-style Shureimon gate to the castle was rebuilt in 1958. The castle itself was completely rebuilt in 1992 according to surviving plans that allowed a restoration to what the castle looked like in the 1700s. The main Seiden Hall, used for state ceremonies by the Ryukyu Kingdom, is the photogenic symbol of the whole castle. The castle serves as a reminder that the Ryukyu Kingdom, founded in 1429, had a unique history and culture, different from that of mainland Japan.

Nakajin Castle

Nakijin Castle was the fortress that controlled the Northern Kingdom of the Ryukyu government. Facing the East China Sea, construction was begun in the 13th century, but remained uncompleted until the early 15th century. This castle, like three others on Okinawa's main island, is enclosed in *gusuku* fortifications. These extensive snake-like enclosures made of limestone follow the contours of the hills they are built on. Remnants of the winding *gusuku* enclosures around Nakajin that survive are 1.6 kilometers long and are entirely different from Japanese castles.

Nakamura Residence

A complex of buildings said to have been built for a village headman in the middle of the 18th century, the Nakamura Residence combines mainland Japanese characteristics and Okinawan architecture. The south side is open to the sun while the other three sides are surrounded by limestone walls.

Eisa

The Eisa Festival in Okinawa is the local equivalent of the Bon festival, which is intended to welcome back the spirits of the ancestors and then see them off again. Local men wearing traditional robes and headgear dance to the beat of *ufudeku* and *shimedeku* drums. The dance itself is said to have originated in the Buddhist Nenbutsu folk dances brought to Okinawa from Japan in the 17th century.

Himeyuri Monument

This monument commemorates the mass suicide of some 200 Okinawan schoolgirls along with their teachers, who chose to stay inside one of the caves used as refuges during the American invasion of the island in 1945.

Katsuren Castle ruins

Like the other castle sites in Okinawa, all that remains of this 15th-century castle are the serpentine stone-wall enclosures made of limestone. Unlike the concave, more angular castle walls of Japanese castles, these fit the contours of the hills upon which the castle once stood. Designated as one of the UNESCO World Heritage Castles of the Ryukyu Kingdom, it was built near the coast and provides a broad view of the surrounding area.

Churaumi Aquarium

The 1975 Expo in Okinawa commemorated the return of Okinawa to Japanese sovereignty. One of the facilities built for the Exposition is now the Okinawa Churaumi Aquarium, which includes an enormous Kuroshio (Black Current) Sea tank, filled with whale sharks and other large fish, and other tanks of tropical fish and specifically Okinawan fish and other sealife. There is also a shark research lab.

Iriomote-jima Island

Iriomote-jima Island is the largest coral reef in Japan, measuring 20 by 15 kilometers. The island is almost completely covered with jungle of mangrove, palm and banyan trees.

Iriomote Yamaneko

The island is famous as the habitat of the Iriomote wild cat. Over 90 percent of the island is covered with subtropical virgin forests.

Yonaguni-jima Island

Yonaguni-jima, the westernmost island of Japan, is a mere 100 kilometers east of Taiwan. In the waters around the island are some huge mysterious structures, the central part of which is some 100 meters in length and 25 meters high. Since their discovery in the 1980s, researchers have sought to determine whether they are some kind of natural landform or the ruins of an ancient civilization that became submerged. Divers and passengers in half-submersible vessels can see the structures on a clear day.

Taketomi-jima Island

A ten-minute boat ride from Ishigaki-jima Island, Taketomi-jima Island is composed completely of coral. Some of the villages have houses with the traditional Okinawan red-tile roofs fixed with white plaster and are surrounded by coral walls. The roads on the island, which has a circumference of nine kilometers, are made of white coral sand, which allows pedestrians to avoid pit vipers on the road at night. During the day, visitors may choose to travel in carts pulled by water buffalo.

Miyako-jima Island

Miyako-jima Island, 300 kilometers southwest of Okinawa Island, is planted with sugar cane and surrounded by white sandy beaches and an emerald green sea. A favorite of divers, swimmers, and triathlon competitors, the island is also known for its ikat handwoven textile known as Miyako jofu.

Hateruma-jima Island

Hateruma-jima Island is the southernmost inhabited island of the country. It is a coral reef sticking out into the ocean, hence its name, which is said to mean "reef at the end of the earth". On the southeast side of the island, along sheer limestone cliffs, is Takana-zaki Point. On the northwest side is a beach protected by sandbars well off-shore. Lying 63 kilometers to the southwest of Ishigaki-jima Island, it is the southernmost inhabited island in Japan.

Hateno-hama Beach, Kume-jima Island

East of Kume-jima Island, a white-sand beach extends some seven to ten kilometers out into the ocean. Three strands of coral sand beach were formed from the remains of coral washed up by waves. The beaches constantly change shape with the movement of the tides and winds.

Imagining Japan
A Memorable Journey

2015年6月6日 第1刷発行
2020年1月24日 第3刷発行

著　　者　　ジェームス・M・バーダマン

発 行 者　　浦　晋亮

発 行 所　　IBCパブリッシング株式会社
　　　　　　〒162-0804
　　　　　　東京都新宿区中里町29番3号
　　　　　　菱秀神楽坂ビル9F
　　　　　　TEL 03-3513-4511
　　　　　　FAX 03-3513-4512
　　　　　　www.ibcpub.co.jp

印 刷 所　　アート印刷株式会社

デザイン　　斉藤啓（ブッダプロダクションズ）

©IBCパブリッシング 2015

落丁本・乱丁本は小社宛にお送りください。
送料小社負担にてお取り替えいたします。
本書の無断複写（コピー）は
著作権法上での例外を除き禁じられています。

ISBN 978-4-7946-0346-3

Printed in Japan

写真：
アフロ（田中秀明、アールクリエイション、小曽納久男、竹下光士、大森通明、堀町政明、藤井吉一、高橋正郎、本橋昂明、千葉直、相澤秀仁＆相澤京子、小谷田整、上野滋數、西垣良次、田上明、Kenneth John Straiton、石井正孝、上甲信男、早山信武、今釜勝良、伊東剛、西野嘉憲、菊地一彦、館野二朗、岡田光司、古岩井一正、田中光常、小早川渉、スタジオサラ、山本つねお、都丸和博、大沢斉、峰脇英樹、楢原光晴、首藤光一、Yuki Kusachi、森田廣美、熊谷公一、Jose Fuste Raga、阿部宗雄、今井悟、田中正秋、高根俊樹、東田裕二、鎌形久、実田謙一、ミヤジシンゴ、片岡巌、山口博之、鐘ヶ江道彦、佐藤尚、山口範之、角田展章、箭内博行、八代洌和、マリンプレスジャパン、小川和夫、山梨将典、清水誠司、川北茂貴、縄手英樹、michio yamauchi、賀輪正、節政博親、萩野矢慶記、市川傳、小川秀一、荒木一紀、富井義夫、山田豊宏、月岡陽一、武藤守、村河敦、石原正雄、佐藤哲郎、加藤省二、前嶋貞男、黒田續生、近藤幹雄、エムオーフォトス、KENJI GOSHIMA、古藤秀二、神原陽一、イメージ・アイ、矢野光則、田中幸男、HIROYUKI OZAWA、大塚武、山梨勝弘、後藤昌美、新海良夫）
© 鹿苑寺 蔵 (p.110)　© 提供慈照寺 (p.111)